JUST WHEN YOU'RE COMFORTABLE IN YOUR OWN SKIN, IT STARTS TO SAG

JUST WHEN YOU'RE COMFORTABLE IN YOUR OWN SKIN, IT STARTS TO SAG

rewriting the rules of midlife

Amy Nobile & Trisha Ashworth

Authors of the Bestseller
I Was a Really Good Mom Before I Had Kids

CHRONICLE BOOKS
SAN FRANCISCO

Copyright © 2018 by Amy Nobile and Trisha Ashworth

All rights reserved. No part of this book may be reproduced in any
form without written permission from the publisher.

Library of Congress Cataloging-in-Publication Data

Names: Nobile, Amy, author. | Ashworth, Trisha, author.
Title: Just when you're comfortable in your own skin, it starts
   to sag : rewriting the rules of midlife / Amy Nobile, Trisha Ashworth.
Description: San Francisco : Chronicle Books, [2018]
Identifiers: LCCN 2017021301 | ISBN 9781452164335 (hc : alk. paper)
Subjects: LCSH: Middle aged women. | Middle age—Psychological aspects. |
   Self-esteem. | Self-realization.
Classification: LCC HQ1059.4 .N63 2018 | DDC 155.6/6—dc23 LC record
available at https://lccn.loc.gov/2017021301

Manufactured in China.

Designed by Tonje Vetleseter

Typesetting by Howie Severson

10 9 8 7 6 5 4 3 2

Chronicle books and gifts are available at special quantity discounts to corporations,
professional associations, literacy programs, and other organizations. For details and
discount information, please contact our premiums department at
corporatesales@chroniclebooks.com or at 1-800-759-0190.

Chronicle Books LLC
680 Second Street
San Francisco, California 94107
www.chroniclebooks.com

We dedicate this book to the Perennials—the pioneers of this generation who are reinventing what it means to be strong, innovative, confident women of any age. A new movement has begun, and we are so grateful that we're forging new ground together. We are uniquely enduring.

CONTENTS

CHAPTER
1

Um, Is This IT?

(Why We Wrote
This Book)

uiz :

You Need
This Book If . . .

- You find yourself second-guessing the choices you've made, and you wonder if you should rethink that . . . job/marriage/ friend thing.

- On a website where you have to indicate the year you were born, it takes a full minute to scroll all the way down to your lucky number.

- You recently bribed your tween to help bolster your Instagram follower count. You feel no shame.

- You go to the same liquor store repeatedly because Bob the (cute-ish) cashier ALWAYS cards you.

- You hire a "spiritual advisor" to see if your next life will be any more exciting.

- You slip the DMV guy $50 to use a younger photo for your driver's license.

- You bully your daughter into agreeing that you have three less wrinkles than Noah's mom.

- You and your husband have some kind of sex schedule you— and he—are mostly satisfied with (and it took only a decade to figure out).

- You feel wiser than ever, and truly don't care what others think of you. (OK, that's true like 30 percent of the time.)

- You're back in the dating pool for the first time in fifteen years. Are there some apps you should be downloading?

- Your hangovers now last seventy-two hours instead of twenty-four.

- You occasionally overstate the age of your kids, just to get compliments about how young you look.

- Overnight, your social calendar is overrun by fortieth and fiftieth birthday parties, instead of weddings and bat mitzvahs.

- That two a.m. phone call is either coming from your kid or your parent. Either way, it ain't pretty.

- The last three items on your bucket list: Trip to India, Feel More Gratitude, and Take a Semi-Decent Selfie.

- You reminisce about how basic, oblivious, and hot you were at twenty-eight.

- You wake up one day unclear of what your true purpose in life is. And you have no f'ing idea how to figure it out.

We know you. You are that woman others always describe as "having it together." By all measures, you guess, it's kind of true. In the past handful of decades, you've ticked some pretty major accomplishments off a list, including, but not limited to: getting a good education, falling in love, falling out of love and surviving, becoming a great friend, crushing it in your work (whether that's coordinating playdates for littles, running a hedge fund, or something in between). You've played by the rules. Maybe you had some kids and learned how to navigate being a mom, being a spouse, and getting just enough yoga, water, and green juice into your days to feel vaguely balanced. You've been a shoulder to cry on for friends and family in need, and you've been there to celebrate every milestone.

So then why, after pushing so hard for so many years, do you feel like you're hitting some kind of . . . plateau? You used to have hobbies, passions, causes. But lately, it seems like all you have are tasks and to-dos, surging hormones, and sagging eyelids. And as you contemplate the next period of your life, you're finding yourself thirsting for more, craving something else—something meaningful, purposeful, but also confusingly absent. You also finally have more time to think about *yourself,* and you're excited about being able to make yourself a priority again in life. It's just that . . . you're not entirely sure *who* that person is at the moment. Or who she's becoming.

You've whispered these confusingly esoteric feelings to a few choice friends, and while they give you an "ohmigod I feel these feelings too" nod and smile, "it" is still tough to articulate, and even tougher to try to solve. The words that swirl in your head boil down to, "Is this not enough? Is . . . this . . . it?"

Take a deep breath.

You are in great company. We feel you. Millions of other women at this Midlife Moment do too. We believe we are at a unique pivot-point in our lives, at a unique time for women in this generation, and we are all uniquely poised to find a new kind of balance and meaning. This book is our way to wrap our arms around the situation, and each other, share some collective wisdom, and find some relief and—hopefully—a few creative ideas and solutions.

A PERSONAL SEARCH FOR OUR OWN NEXT SOMETHING

We are fast and forever best friends, collaborators, entrepreneurs, creatives, dedicated spouses, and (not last, definitely not least) moms. After writing three best-selling books about motherhood and marriage and producing a TV show for Lifetime, we should have been feeling pretty fulfilled.

But despite having seemingly everything one might need to lead a happy, full life, we were finding ourselves struggling with our own relevance, grappling with our own feelings of fulfillment. Even after writing several successful books, we were failing to

"It's scary—you don't know what the story now looks like. I always knew the story before."

Shelly, 49
CHICAGO, IL

appreciate the moment and enjoy the time. We were too busy wondering what was coming next. And with every new idea we had, we heard "Ohhhh no, you can't do THAT" from all angles, which became exhausting.

We knew we were lucky enough to have the time to even question how we were feeling. Our lives looked perfect to many. We live in nice homes and can afford to take vacations, for which we are incredibly thankful. We've been on stage with Oprah. We have healthy kids, who are by all measures headed on the right paths; we have supportive and successful husbands; we have all four limbs and good heads (and hair!) on our shoulders; we have semi-functioning households; we have our mental and physical health situations largely under control.

"You can't create a life plan. I never would have imagined myself forty-seven years old and divorced with a kid."

Shauna, 47
STUART, FL

But like everyone else, there have been so many days—and there continue to be days!—when we struggle to keep our heads above water and to live up to our own expectations. On one day, we'll berate ourselves for "failing" our children, our spouses, ourselves. The next day, our kids will shockingly announce to us that we did something right. That they maybe kinda appreciate us. They see what we've done for them, and they're grateful.

All this is to say, we're human.

And yet, throughout this emotional ping-pong, we noticed we were entering a stage where, all of a sudden, we were feeling more and more like there was something big still missing. It was hard to articulate what that something was. And truth be told, we even felt a little guilty for admitting to ourselves—and each other—that we were a little lost.

Here we were, our kids in their preteens and teens, our parents growing older, our friends reappearing after a long absence, our days stretching before us, and we found ourselves wondering something pretty major: What was this Next Chapter meant to look like? You know, that vast twenty-year period between mid-late motherhood and retirement? No one had really ever talked to us about what happens after your kids stop needing you every five minutes, after you've kind of figured out that new role. And no one told us we'd be questioning not only what our futures looked like but who we are now.

We finally had a little more time, our stiletto-sharp wits still intact, and yet, we had no compelling model for what we should be doing with ourselves. Were we seriously meant to go into a black hole and reemerge with sexy gray bobs, playing mah-jongg and nagging our grandchildren to "like" us on Facebook?

THE QUESTIONS WE ARE QUIETLY ASKING OURSELVES:

◊ How do I find balance?

◊ How do I find purpose—and what does that even mean?

◊ What is my true passion—and how do I find it?

◊ What does happiness mean now?

◊ What does success mean to me?

> "On paper I had it all. The dream job—I was 'successful'—I did everything I was supposed to do. But at the core, I didn't really know who I was. I wasn't fully present, at my core, in my life. There was some-thing palpable, tangible, that I knew I had to uncover in myself."
>
> **Jana, 42**
> TRAVERSE CITY, MI

◇   What do I want my legacy to look like?

◇   Who am I becoming?

◇   Are all of these questions . . . normal?

We craved a next act. We craved meaning, fulfillment, community, and yes, some fun. We craved having clarity about what this was all supposed to look like, and license to do it in a totally new way. We were excited, scared, and frankly, flailing.

WE ARE NOT ALONE

On a whim, we decided to take a trip together to Haiti. And that experience, magically and miraculously, was the first step in what has become an important part of our journey. The trip was a humanitarian one; one day we met up with artisans making beautiful jewelry out of natural resources. We were inspired in so many ways. Months later, our company ASH + AMES was born. It was not an obvious move for us; never in a million years did we think this would have been our path. But as we traveled around Haiti—a country whose people are incredibly gentle and generous despite the poverty that engulfs them—and processed our own questions about what was right for our next chapter, we decided to open ourselves up to the unknown. We decided to marshal our courage and commit to putting ourselves out there, and yes, dream a dream.

The process we took to get there involved a lot of work. Uncovering our passion and building a company was our own self-help process. And after having

"Somehow having kids threw me into type A overdrive—I made a birth plan, a nutrition plan, a nursery school plan, a college plan . . . but in the midst of it all, I completely forgot about myself. I woke up recently and realized now that my kids are pretty much on their own, I HAVE NO PLAN! How is that even possible??"

Anna, 39
DETROIT, MI

opened ourselves up, we were wowed by the opportunity and excitement we found when we pushed ourselves past the feelings of paralysis and fear. We had an idea, visualized our path, applied a laser focus to getting there, and tuned out all that extra noise, the inner and outer critics. Our goal was to enable a new generation of female entrepreneurs, by giving women a way to launch their next chapters, while also doing something for the larger good.

We began interviewing prospective "Ambassadors," independent businesswomen who would sell jewelry through their networks. What started as interviews ended up sparking a much deeper conversation, one we extended with hundreds more women across the country as we reported this book. We talked to women of all walks of life—longtime urban executives, single moms in the suburbs, recently divorced women figuring out what's next for them, women sending their kids off to college, women who had firmly and happily decided kids were never for them. We talked to women who had stepped off the work treadmill twenty years ago and were trying to find a way back on. We talked to women who were frustrated with their partners and trying to figure out whether to finally do something about it and invest in their own happiness.

What we found surprised us.

The women spoke of feeling newly confident in their own skin. They spoke of feeling a vague hunger for something "more," but what that was they couldn't yet identify. They spoke of entering a new

"I want to use my brain, be productive, contribute to society and my family. I'm at that gap age—I'm midforties but not old. With these remaining working years, what do I want to be doing?"

Cindy, 44
DENVER, CO

"I am where I thought I'd be. And part of me is disappointed."
Mary, 44 NEW CASTLE, DE

"I think I assumed that I'd reach a point of natural 'fulfillment' at this time in my life. It's like I've checked every box—and am coming up short in terms of the way these things—like getting my kids into good schools, or having the house I've always wanted—make me feel. Is it even okay for me to ask for more?"
Kelly, 40 BOSTON, MA

"I'm confident finally—even if my ass is big."
Kathy, 39 SYRACUSE, NY

"I feel like for the first time, I'm becoming myself. Not a daughter and a wife. I am bubbling to the surface now. I'm in the bold letters. It's just ME. It's sort of terrifying and exhilarating."
Shelly, 49 CHICAGO, IL

phase in their relationships (with their husbands, their kids, their friends). They spoke of fears, dreams, hopes. Mostly, they spoke of not having a road map to follow. Across every conversation, one thing was consistent and clear: our mothers may have entered this stage of life looking at it as a LOSS. But that was not ringing true for us. This was not our mothers' midlife crisis. In fact, this was not a crisis at all.

These women are opening a new chapter, looking forward, and they are driven by hope and opportunity. Everyone we talked to seemed to be grappling with their search for the next something. In many cases, they talked about feeling some sort of strange void, but couldn't put their finger on what it was. These were successful, highly educated, passionate, accomplished, wonderful women—lawyers, teachers, marketing professionals, personal organizers, moms.

The interviews quickly evolved into cathartic therapy sessions all centered around women feeling lost—wondering where to go next and what their paths should be now that they had the previous stage of their life seemingly under control. And while we were hearing a lot of the same words coming out of women's mouths, everyone was talking about feeling *alone*.

Over the course of writing our three books, we've been on a journey connecting with women and surfacing their innermost needs. We've interviewed hundreds of women each time, and each of our books tracked with our previous stages of life: marriage, motherhood, and more. We united millions of women in a movement to tell their own personal truths on

> "It seems as though the clock started winding down once our moms hit midlife. For us, we're just hitting the 'restart' button."
>
> **Dina, 40**
> HOUSTON, TX

Oprah. And with each stage, we heard themes, uncovered generational complexities, and helped women find solace and solutions.

And now, here we are again, a decade later, hearing similar themes from hundreds more women, hungering for the same things we had been feeling ourselves. Right in step, we were unearthing a real, tangible need for help in navigating this next phase.

The women we talked to expected that, since they'd checked the neat and tidy boxes off their list of expectations from earlier in life—whether around motherhood, careers, relationships—they'd feel fulfilled, happy, and at peace with their lives as they entered this next phase. But they didn't feel that way, and neither did we.

WE ARE A NEW GENERATION

We looked to the logical place for insights: our moms. However, as much as we wish this weren't true, we couldn't imagine following their paths. Amy's mom and stepdad divorced as soon as Amy turned eighteen, and her mom was thrown into the workforce for the first time in her life at age thirty-six. Her mom had never gone to college and, because of her circumstances, she wasn't really given permission to have big dreams of her own. She found her way by securing a job at a prestigious law firm, where she's still diligently working to this day. In part this drove Amy's decision to become a working mom—so that she'd always have an active career to fall back on—which came with its own set of intense and unexpected challenges.

"My mom was a great woman—she just didn't have permission to be what she wanted to be beyond motherhood. She didn't ever talk about it."

Sophie, 38
PORTLAND, OR

Trisha's mom stayed at home with her and her siblings, and Trisha followed in her stead. That's what good moms do, right? And they certainly don't prioritize their own happiness, needs, or emotions above the family.

Other women we talked to had similar questions about whether the paths their mothers followed would fulfill them throughout their lives, or whether the road maps their mothers showed them were ones they could really envision following.

Our moms did not celebrate or embrace midlife, they simply suffered through it; and as we approach our own midlife, they don't feel like the right role models for us. We're left feeling unprepared . . . and at odds with how to reinvent ourselves.

The women we talked to were all well aware that our generation is different—we benefit from great advantages. We have access to all kinds of interesting jobs; sharing responsibilities at home is now very much the norm. And we're lucky to have the choices we do. All is at our fingertips, the glass ceiling has been broken, the options are limitless. What we lack is direction.

◇ We're dealing with aging parents and kids—and ourselves—all at once. It's a perfect storm. (This feels very different from our moms' generation, that convergence of issues.)

◇ There are more pressures/expectations to have it all.

◇ We're more in touch with our kids and reflective about how we were at their age. (And we'll happily discuss how messed up we were at their ages.)

◇ Two-income households are increasingly the norm.

◇ We're aware of our inner feelings and open to therapy.

◇ We're supposed to seem completely chill while having it all.

◇ Looking, feeling, and acting younger longer is the norm.

◇ We're having kids older.

◇ We believe we deserve happiness and we will do what it takes to get there.

A compliment
THEN

You are such an
amazing mom!

Honey, you
look hot!

You did a great job
on that project!

Are you seriously
not 22?!

You could
balance a plate
on your ass.

A compliment
NOW

You do not
look like you had
three kids!

Honey, you look
the same as you
did at 32!

You have the
energy of a
32-year-old!

Are you seriously
not 32?

Everything about
you is balanced!

YOU CAN'T DENY GRAVITY

While all of that turmoil was swirling on the inside, it was all too easy to overlook what was happening on the outside. We noticed that the answer to "What's the best compliment you could receive?" had shifted. For our first book, the best compliment was unanimously "You are a good mom." A close second was "Were those cupcakes you brought to the bake sale homemade?" (No . . . but still, we'll take it.)

This time, across the board—and we know this may sound crazy given the amazing qualities we've all accrued over the years—we want to hear that *we look younger than we actually are*. Although this may seem like vanity, it's a very real feeling—the pressure that we sense (from ourselves and others and the media) to look and feel younger than we are, to do everything we can to slow the passing of time. And as if feeling bad about our bodies isn't enough, we're supposed to feel bad about feeling bad? Maybe we should start feeling bad about feeling bad about feeling bad?

On the one hand, while we want to feel and seem younger, in many ways we're coming to a place of self-awareness, acceptance, and even appreciation when it comes to our bodies. We are increasingly becoming more comfortable and confident with ourselves, and that's great! All those quirks and flaws we've struggled with, apologized for, and tried to cover up are now just out there.

REFRAMING HAPPINESS AND SUCCESS

The other question that literally stumped the women we talked with was "What does success look like for you now?" That word—success—was weighty and perplexing. It was obvious the women we were talking with hadn't spent time really thinking about what success means for them. Success was a word we all used—and pointed ourselves toward—but it lacked clear and consistent meaning.

For some, success means getting a promotion and a dedicated assistant. For others, success is a matter of getting the kids into the right schools and summer camps and afterschool classes and playdates. But those accomplishments didn't seem to add up to *feelings* of success. Women we talked to didn't feel particularly "good" at anything, since they'd been stretched so thin for so long. They also felt embarrassed by their reaction to the word and their inability to articulate what it truly meant to them.

Unlike success, happiness isn't something we are specifically told to strive for, and yet we all seem to find ourselves grasping for it, and filling our days with activities geared to helping us find it. All those yoga classes, cleanses, therapist sessions, self-help books, subscriptions to O, meditation apps. We're doing anything and everything we can to soul-search our way to true happiness and peace within ourselves.

"There's a fundamental change happening. With my family, yes, and my kids, my body, my wrinkles ...you can't deny gravity. It's there, it's real."

Shelly, 49
CHICAGO, IL

AVOIDING THE ISSUE

When everything outwardly is going so right for us all, it's pretty confusing to feel like something is missing. And since we don't know what exactly is missing, it's hard to know how to fill that void. Picking up piano again, getting a regular tennis game going, learning how to make paella on the grill. Those are some of the healthier choices women we talked to made.

Then there are other, more extreme (and not always healthy) methods some of us are happily choosing to fill that void:

1   Having another baby

2   Filling another prescription

3   Gutting and redesigning the kitchen

4   Developing a marriage-testing addiction to Bravo

5   Going back to school

THE SLIDING SCALE

The reality is that we're all on some kind of sliding scale showing where we "sit" in this moment. At the bottom, some of us are feeling just a little lost, while some of us with quite a few issues (internal and external) converging at once are hovering in the middle. And some of us are at the top, in straight-up crisis mode, dealing with faulty marriages, aging parents, and crazy teenagers. The common thread as we deal with all these issues is that we're reevaluating

"I feel as happy as I can given all the other stresses in my life. One of the ways I find progress and happiness is by determining how I'm handling myself and hard times. That goes really far in giving me *peace*."

Amy, 47
GREENBRAE, CA

where we are and redefining the next chapters, on our own terms.

Whether it's a "gnawing," a "void," a "need," a "hunger," we use different words to describe the feelings we're experiencing. Some women are feeling truly paralyzed at this time . . . while some feel that there's just something "not quite right" or just a little off. Some of us aren't even sure that there's something missing—but once we hear our friends mention it, we become keenly aware of our own void and the cravings to fill it.

> *"I drink a LOT of wine. How much is a lot? I have a goal every night: I DON'T GO BELOW THE LABEL. I just keep pouring a little bit at a time."*

True Confession:

The fact is, however we experience or describe it—and wherever we sit on the scale—feeling that void is real. And recognizing it is unsettling for a lot of us. But once we open up and give ourselves permission to really investigate our feelings, we realize there's something deeper going on and that the void is actually a big, gaping opportunity to fill our lives with something WE get to choose. That next chapter is ours to write.

And write it we must. Amid the swirl of dealing with aging parents and teens, we can't revert to

"It's like there was an uncomfortable 'gnawing'—or knowing that there was so much more. My choices at the time were to either numb it out—keep going through the motions—or seek out a solution that would get me more grounded in who I was, and what my ultimate goals were."

Jana, 42
NEW YORK, NY

that familiar behavior of deprioritizing ourselves for everyone else. Sure, work and marital issues are the *perfect* excuse to leave ourselves off the priority list, but if we want to honor our own selves and push the vision we have for the future forward, sometimes we need to force ourselves to take that first step.

FINDING COMMUNITY AGAIN

When our kids were little, it was so easy to find other people at the same stage. You could spot your sleep-deprived soulmate at a playground, or lock eyes with a similarly time-strapped mom across a conference room table. There were mom-dates, playgroups, boot camps, soccer games, double-parent dates your husband outwardly dreaded—any number of excuses to get together with other women. And we didn't just crave it—we lived for it.

But now, as we forge into this new zone, it's less obvious how we find each other, commiserate, and talk through and laugh about our shared experiences—newly sprouting gray hair, tweenage angst, hot flashes, and more.

Finding our community at this moment isn't exactly the most natural thing. Where are you supposed to pick people up? Your dermatologist's waiting room?

SO WHY DO WE FEEL THIS WAY?

As we talked to hundreds of women of all stripes, we heard consistent themes you'll see us explore in the coming chapters.

"We are on this journey together, and there's less labeling. There's an openness to what is possible for all of us, which is exciting."

Sienna, 39
RENO, NV

◇ There's a brand-new archetype. We're no longer just SAH moms or working moms. We're a hybrid.

◇ We don't look or feel or act like our parents did at forty and fifty and beyond.

◇ We're educated, passionate, mission-driven women.

◇ We've lost a critical sense of belonging and community at this age.

◇ We are not our mothers—reinvention is a new concept for us in midlife.

◇ Success was more easily defined for our moms. It's not defined for us.

◇ We've buried ourselves in motherhood for so long—it was an acceptable excuse to not deal with our wants and our future paths.

◇ We're grieving the life we built—the sense of clarity and forward motion we had just a few years back.

◇ We're caught up in living lives based on the expectations of others—not what we necessarily want.

◇ We're feeling forced to reevaluate where we were, where we are, and where we're going.

WRITING OUR OWN PLANS

We are women with a clear plan and organized framework for absolutely everything—birthday parties, ACT test prep, restocking the freezer, the next four summer vacations—and yet, somehow, here we are without a "Life Plan" for ourselves!

That changes here and now. This is the book that will help you feel less alone, understand how and why our generation of women is facing a totally unique stage, and reimagine it for what it is—a pivot-point to embrace our new confidence, think proactively about what we want, and give ourselves all the permission we need to go out and get it. A reinvention of yourself, if you will. We like the idea of using the term "Perennials" to describe our generation—we are ever evolving, enduring, and vibrant.

We're here to provide acknowledgment of what you're going through, a spirit of acceptance, and a set of tools that have actually worked for others. We're here to share in our experience with you, where we can hear each other out, find tangible and real relief, laugh together, and ultimately create a community of true sisterhood.

"It used to be you had a moms' group for working through this kind of stuff. And now here we are at this next phase—and there's no support group!!"

Sheila, 48
DUXBURY, MA

OVER THE NEXT SIX CHAPTERS, THIS BOOK WILL
HELP YOU:

◇ Figure out who you want to be when you grow up

◇ Prioritize yourself and ask yourself some tough
questions about what you really want

◇ Break through the fears that are holding you back

◇ Sort through potential opportunities/dreams

◇ Find (or reimagine) your purpose and passion

◇ Redefine "middle age"/redefine what it means to
be "our age"

◇ Think about what it means to live the life you want,
on your own terms

◇ Proactively OWN your next chapter(s)

◇ Readjust expectations and break the rules (go back to
school/grow long hair/dress the way you want)

◇ Let go of those expectations of who you thought
you were

◇ Reengage in meaningful endeavors with
meaningful people

◇ Feel less alone

CHAPTER

2

Balancing an Eighteen-Year-Old and a Seventy-Eight-Year-Old

(Entering the Perfect Storm)

Quiz :

Which of the Following is Part of Your Reality?
(check all that apply)

- You have a teenager with some seriously raging hormones.

- You have some seriously raging hormones. (!)

- You are dating again for the first time.

- Your marriage (along with your body) is sagging.

- The career you've been working at for decades isn't as fulfilling as you thought it would be.

- In the past year, you bought diapers for both a parent and a child.

- In the past few months, you've lost a friend, relative, or pet.

- You feel a little twinge in your back/shoulder/knee, but we're not going to talk about it. Twinges are for old people.

- That nightly glass of wine has turned into a half bottle, and you start thinking about it at 4:30 p.m.

- You feel increasingly unsettled.

- Your savings is not what you'd hoped it would be.

- That anxiety you've been successfully medicating for years is now less predictable.

- You feel like you're in an unexpected tornado and not sure how you got here.

- You keep procrastinating about . . . doing anything for YOU. (OR After all these years, you're STILL not on your priority list.)

- What "those parents" said really is true—parenting kids as they get older really does not get easier.

- You desperately wish for parents you could turn to now for advice, or just a hug.

Did you check at least four? Congratulations! You are in great company. Welcome to the club you didn't sign up for.

We like to think we're on top of it all. That we can handle whatever comes our way. That we've *got* this. The truth is, we do have this. We have it all, and then some— the aging parents, the aging teens, the aging selves, the seasoned (or broken or absent) marriages, the shifting bodies, the shifting careers. And it's all happening right now.

Part of the problem is that women of our generation are overachievers. We like to be stars at all that we do. We want to be everything to everyone:

◇ the loving mom

◇ the patient child

◇ the wise friend

◇ the thoughtful spouse

◇ the seasoned professional

◇ the good cook

◇ the Instagram pro

◇ the generous neighbor

◇ the collaborative colleague

At the very bottom of the list, we hesitantly allow ourselves to add one more person: ourselves. But only after we've taken care of everyone else, and checked all those other boxes. And when we do attend to ourselves, it's to attempt to tighten the bod, smooth the lines, dress the part. We want trim waistlines, fat bank balances, centered minds.

Looking inward and feeding the soul tends to come absolutely last, if ever. We often don't realize or acknowledge that what we're taking on is just not sane or healthy. It is unfortunately normal, but that doesn't make it okay.

YOU ARE PART OF SOMETHING

So much of what those of us at this stage are facing, this perfect storm, is new for us and our friends. Our parents may have dealt with some or all of these issues, but they certainly never had to deal with them during their own midlife mashup, all at once. Even if we rationally know all this is coming, we feel blindsided when we realize that things get more stressful in midlife. We were sold visions that aren't coming true. We're not watching the clock as we head toward a timeshare in Scottsdale for a boring and blissful retirement. We're not crawling into a weepy fetal position to mourn the departure of our children as they move on up and out (well, it's tougher for some of us than others). We're certainly not going gray and wrinkled as part of a political display of our feminist feelings. Our approach is more complicated, more nuanced, more . . . Midlife 2.0.

SO WHAT'S DIFFERENT FOR US?

We're having kids older. All those years we spent in our twenties finding love, ourselves, our careers—and not having kids yet. Thank god we did all that then, but in many ways, we're paying the price now as all things collide.

Elder care is better now, so our aging parents are sicker (or healthy-ish) longer. While we're able to sustain our lives longer, we're caring for our aging parents at precisely the same time we're dealing with our kids' most challenging years. Our folks are around longer, which is both a blessing and (yes, we'll say it) an occasional curse. And even if they're on the healthier side, we are the ones caring for them emotionally and making some life-altering decisions on their behalf.

We feel increased pressure to be superwomen/supermoms. We are the champions of taking it all on. Throughout our lives, we have been the efficient and happy coordinators. We are the master of ceremonies, pulling together parties, get-togethers, our careers, our homes, our health and wellness appointments, travel plans. By now we should have it all together and things are meant to get easier, since we should be seasoned and accomplished life professionals. If only that were the case. New challenges are being put on our superwoman plates and we feel unequipped to handle it all. With careers, kids, and parents colliding, it can feel overwhelming and lead to frustration, if not despair.

"Women are primarily responsible for providing care for kids and elderly parents, which ends up derailing their careers!

"There's a huge difference between care-giving for your parent and caring for your child. For your parent, there's a continual downhill slide. I'm guiding my mother to her death."

Marcy, 45
BATESVILLE, AK

I've seen this happen again and again. Divorce, death, husbands losing their jobs—it's the women who pay the price for providing care for everyone else. I'm hearing so many women say: I'm nowhere in my career and have to support myself and my kids for the next twenty years—what am I going to do?"—Angela Tripoli, life coach

We are used to having plans for ourselves and we feel lost. On both sides of us, there is great movement. Our kids' worlds are expanding and growing. Our parents' worlds are shrinking and narrowing. While we deal with both sides, and stand in the middle of two opposite-moving walkways, it can feel like we are stagnating while getting tugged in opposite directions.

We like to be in control, and we feel like we're losing it. Let's face it. Over the past twenty to thirty years, we've done a damn good job of keeping everything together. We love being in control, and we're good at it. Now, all of a sudden, it feels like that sense of control is slipping out of our fingers, and it's confusing! Even when it comes to our own aging and mortality, we're trying to find little things we can do to assert our control. We even have a friend who created a spreadsheet outlining everything she would want at her funeral (she's forty-six!), from her choice of bubbly to music to the guest list. At first we thought it sounded a little morbid, but she was dead serious.

EVERYTHING YOU STILL HAVE UNDER CONTROL (THANK YOU VERY MUCH)

◇ The organization of apps on your smartphones

◇ Short list of foods that don't make you bloated

- Friends' and family members' birthdays (digital tools save the day)

- Vacation ideas for next summer (and people you actually want to travel with)

- All of your passwords for websites (ignore the fact that you use the same three over and over)

- A thirty-minute exercise routine that's just heart-pumping enough

- Sending out holiday cards in time for Martin Luther King Day

- The foresight to cancel newspapers before going out of town

We are no longer part of a tribe living close together. Our moms had their bridge friends, their neighbors, their oldest of friends, not to mention their families nearby. In our post-college, early motherhood, career-building, and marriage stages, we had other moms from school, colleagues, old friends. Now it seems our closest friends from our twenties and thirties, while still treasured, are so spread out. As we are wrestling with new, complicated, internal feelings, as we enter this big new transition, we need our tribe more than ever, and it is farther from reach.

Barry Schwartz, the author of *The Paradox of Choice* and an emeritus professor of psychology at Swarthmore College, sees all of these competing needs as a moment of great opportunity, if only because it can create a powerful sense of purpose. "What saves people is that their circumstances in life constrain them. If you

"As an adult, when you lose a parent you start to look at your life in a different way. Instead of looking at the past, you look at the future and the time you have left."

Cynthia, 55
CONCORD, CA

"Just in the last ten years, between ages forty-two and fifty-one, I had two jobs, I started my own company, my kids went from seven and ten to being college bound, and I hit this midlife journey. At the beginning it was simpler, and then, as they entered their teen years and then neared college, both my parents got sick and died. My mom just passed away in early August, and then I had to take my first kid to college. The month of August was this overwhelming feeling of *loss*."
Sarah, 52 STUDIO CITY, CA

"You had a mom's group when the kids were little . . . and here we are at this next phase . . . and there's NO support group!"
Grace, 50 PRINCETON, NJ

"I think we look at midlife as a conundrum. Our moms just had a 'crisis.' Now it's 'Oh shit! What am I going to do next?' There's more of an emphasis on having meaningful work. Our parents didn't think that way."
Mila, 39 BEND, OR

have aging parents and older kids—this is a burden, and also tells you what to do every morning. There's nothing much more terrifying than a blank canvas and an abyss of choice. When you're not needed anymore by your kids—it's really hard. You think, 'Now what?'"

DECISIONS AND TRANSITIONS

There's no doubt that we've been capable of making good and strong decisions throughout our lives. We've landed pretty squarely on our feet. We have finally gotten to a place where we know what ticks us off and what turns us on; we have our signature cocktails and scents. We're accomplished and confident and together, at least outwardly.

But the decisions we're facing right now are professional grade and would crush even the strongest among us.

◇ **Should I stay married?**

◇ **Where should I send my kid to college? (Am I comfortable draining the savings/taking out monster loans for private school?)**

◇ **Do I abandon the career I've worked so hard for to follow my dream?**

◇ **How should I help my parent die?**

◇ **What do I want for myself in the next ten years?**

These are not matters meant to be taken lightly. There are no right answers. And there's certainly no clear path to follow. The result? We can be left feeling passionless, purposeless, and completely stressed out.

"When I was younger, I had roommates and a gaggle of friends. And back when we were young moms, maybe we grabbed a glass of wine. Now it's a downward slope. There's so much less time to spend talking openly and honestly. There are so many taboo topics, like having a tough time with your husband, that you try to navigate around. And I have to admit I'm afraid of being judged for what I'm going through."

Kate, 47
BOULDER, CO

The transitions we're facing are significant: death of family members, emptying the nest, breakups, career moves. Just one of those alone would be cause for some serious introspection and reflection. And adding to the complication is that our partners are also going through their own midlife transitions—at the very same time. We want to help them, but their stress and agitation only adds to ours. And we feel like we need to put on our oxygen masks before we can help anyone else.

At this point, based on where we are in our journeys, a lot of this is happening at the same time. And it's stirring up a whole cocktail of complicated feelings:

◇ Joy
◇ Fear
◇ Excitement
◇ Dread
◇ Sorrow

◇ Escapism
◇ Regret
◇ Wanderlust
◇ Anxiety

> "If we looked at midlife like a teen, we'd take risks, connect with friends, get more in touch with our feelings, explore our options and possibilities."
>
> Dana, 49
> SONOMA, CA

True Confession:

"I sometimes forget how old I am— does that make me old?"

◆

TAKING ON THE TABOO

Part of the biggest challenge in all this is that it's so easy to feel isolated, lonely, maybe even quietly (or openly!) judged. At different times in life, there are feelings, questions, and thoughts that are totally taboo. After talking to hundreds of women around the country, we can confidently say we're all wondering about and struggling with the same issues. And it can be freeing to shine some bright light on what's swirling around in our heads, to make us all feel just a little less guilty, less judged—and find some quality company.

Age	Taboo Questions
In your twenties	How much do you make?
In your thirties	How much sex do you actually have?
In your forties	Are you happy?
In your fifties	Are you fulfilled?

There . . . we said it. Actually, *you* said it, in great confidence, and in great numbers. We're all out with it. Now let's start to say it to ourselves and each other, so we can acknowledge that many of us are feeling similar things and we're all in this together.

> "As I get older, I try to keep things to myself. I'm afraid of judgment—'C'mon, you haven't worked for so many years, you're so lucky!' Do people really not understand that it's a choice I've made to be a stay-at-home mom? Even my son has judgment. 'Mom, you should get a job!'"
>
> **Kathy, 51**
> NEW YORK, NY

◇ I'm a fraud and people are going to find me out.

◇ I don't think I'm a very good partner/mom/person.

◇ I don't really like my husband very much.

◇ My kids frustrate me.

◇ I don't know who I am and who I want to be.

◇ I often think, "Is this IT??"

◇ I don't want to be responsible for taking care of my parents.

◇ I wish I had more money.

◇ I'm scared of dying.

MAYBE THOSE CRAZY KIDS ARE ONTO SOMETHING

Despite how insane and irrational they can sometimes seem, teenagers have a few things to teach us about transitional moments. One of us (Amy) has a teenage son who went through an especially challenging time during his seventh-grade year. He was in desperate pain in a way she couldn't solve. If your kid breaks a leg, you put a cast on it. But this? As self-proclaimed perfectionists and control freaks, we're used to pulling every lever we can find to solve our kids' problems, but sometimes the issue can feel *unsolvable*. He didn't like himself very much, and his pain was torturous for everyone in the family.

We shared with him one of our favorite books, *The Four Agreements: A Practical Guide to Personal Freedom* by Don Miguel Ruiz. It's something we've turned to over the years, and it served him well in this moment. One of the lessons of the book is about not taking things personally. For example: When you walk into a room, how do you remain present and give what you can give, without relying on how others respond to you?

This really made an impression on Amy's son, and watching him digest this fresh insight was powerful for everyone. Now he'll turn to her occasionally and say, "Mom, why did you just agree to that? You think you have to be everything to everyone. Don't take things personally; this is not about you."

Yes, teenagers are largely out of control themselves. They are in a state of searching, and they have a lot to learn. But we do too, and if we look at a few ways they are navigating their own personal pivot points, if we watch them absorb some of this information with bright and open eyes, we can learn so much from them.

Teens experience so many shifts and metamorphoses going from childhood to adulthood—and they often find deeper levels of self-awareness and perspective. They're learning who they are, in real time, in front of our eyes. They're going through identity struggles, within themselves and between each other.

Sounds pretty familiar, right?

FOUR KEY THINGS WE COULD LEARN FROM TEENAGERS:

1   How to be more selfish. Teens know how to put themselves first. And they don't apologize for it.

2   A wide-eyed "why *not* me?" attitude. There's beauty in the combination of confidence and ignorance.

3   Self-acceptance around changing shape. It's okay to be one thing one day and something else the next. Teens don't feel the need to be solidified and sure of themselves. They know it's okay to be learning as they go, to be vulnerable, to change shape unapologetically.

4   The importance of friendship and social life in self-discovery. Teens center their lives around their network. They learn who they are through being with others. They prioritize their friends above all.

Part of the problem with entering this new moment is that the words we have to use feel so off. Seriously, is "midlife" all we have? Is there a single person who wants to embrace that state of purgatory? It's neither here nor there, neither young nor old, neither this nor that. Not only is "midlife" bland and nondescript, it fails to capture the full spirit of where we are and the nuance of what we're feeling. As one woman shared with us, "The word 'midlife' just feels CRAZY. When someone asks me how old I am, my mind goes to thirty." Another woman had a simple description of the word "midlife": "gross."

While we're all about embracing the stage we're at, we certainly don't need to celebrate the word we've been given to describe it. Instead of just going with "midlife," we asked hundreds of women what they'd prefer to call it. We spent countless hours interviewing women all over the country and are firm believers in calling things as they should be, articulating the value of something in a way to make it feel both accurate and true. Here are some bright ideas YOU came up with for rebranding midlife, straight from your own mouths.

◆ ALTERNATIVES TO " MIDLIFE" ◆

◇ Rebirth

◇ Better half

◇ Prime time

◇ Bliss

◇ My life

◇ Kindergarten 2.0

◇ Awakening

◇ Becoming

◇ What's possible

◇ Perennial phase

FULL LIVES, FULL HOUSE, FULL HEARTS

"Forty was tough for me. I was pregnant with my second, so I was in midlife AND pregnant. I felt like it was the end of life. Between my job and traveling and the kids, it was isolating not seeing my girlfriends. Now at forty-six I see the light at the end of the tunnel. I can go back to work, start traveling again."

Caroline, 46
Southfield, MI

If in our twenties and thirties we were building the foundation of our lives, in our forties and fifties we have a full house. Many generations are with us sharing the space. And we can't really relax just yet. The building is showing signs of deterioration, the roof needs a bit of work, the floors could definitely be refinished, we need a few more chairs at the family table, and someone left the front door open.

We can see that things will quiet down soon, that we will be able to sit and read a good novel in our favorite chaise, maybe take a bath with some great beauty products. But we're not quite there yet.

The house will soon be more comfortable and quiet. And we will fill the space with laughter and friends and food and yoga mats and bottles of wine and maybe our partners too—as long as they're going to help clean up at the end of the day.

It will be wonderful.

EIGHT EASY STEPS TO SURVIVING THE PERFECT STORM
(WITH JUST A MODICUM OF GRACE)

1. Reconnect with a few key friends going through the same transitions and commit to a call or a date at least once a month.

2. Consider your expectations of yourself in this moment. Do you think anyone else would be able to do all that you expect of yourself?

3. Acknowledge your deepest fears about where you are in your life: Is it being alone? Losing a loved one? Losing control? Air that worry to a friend so you can put it out in the universe. It will be so much less scary.

4. Think of all of the things in your life that are *not* changing. What are some things you are happy to have remain the same?

5. Develop some self-care routines you can tap into when things get especially challenging. It could be meditation, deep breathing, a regular evening walk. Put them in your calendar— and honor them.

6. Allow yourself the room to ask for what you want, whether that is alone time, quiet company, or a raucous night out.

7. Let your partner be your partner. Ask for help. Be okay with not totally being yourself and in control. There can be something so freeing about letting yourself be vulnerable in this turbulent sea.

8. Reconnect to your core values. This is different from your competencies. Are you a nurturing person? Does inner peace hinge on spending time in nature? Prioritize what elements in your life need the most attention, and focus on how you can best serve those areas.

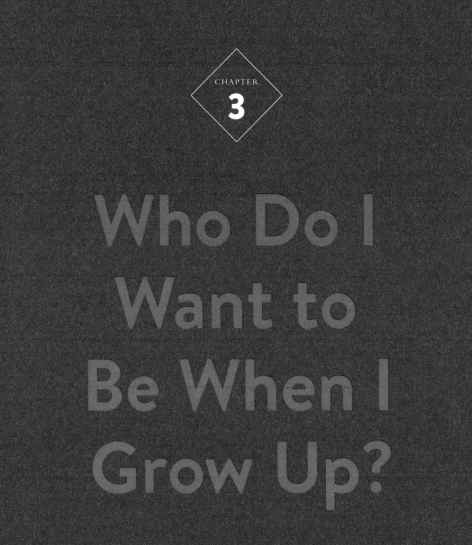

Who Do I Want to Be When I Grow Up?

(Aligning Expectations
and Reality)

Quiz :

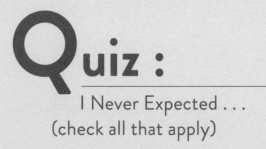

I Never Expected . . .
(check all that apply)

- ◆ To ask for a tampon from my child.

- ◆ To get an AARP brochure in the mail.

- ◆ To feel sexier now than fifteen years ago, even with that extra cushion around the waist.

- ◆ To look down at my hands and literally not recognize them.

- ◆ To relate to my mother.

- ◆ To be creating a Tinder account, for the first time, at this age.

- ◆ To completely change careers.

- ◆ To feel invisible.

- To have pimples *again*.

- To feel 100 percent good about having a little "work" done, and keeping it a secret.

- To feel so confident.

- To love the freedom that comes with not giving a f*ck what anyone else thinks.

- To feel more anxiety now than I've ever felt in my life.

- To be questioning everything in my life, including my marriage.

- To feel exhilarated about what the second half of my life will reveal.

Surprised by how many boxes you checked? Us too. This stage continues to surprise us, every day. Didn't expect to be newly single in your forties? Didn't expect to never have found "the one" and finding yourself increasingly comfortable with being solo? Never imagined yourself as the mother of teenagers? Never could have predicted the amount of money you secretly spend on personal upkeep?

While none of those things were to be expected, they're all here for many of us. Generationally, we're trying to sort out our expectations of what "midlife" looks and feels like for us. It's inherently and categorically different from what our own mothers experienced.

YOUR LIFE, IN FOUR PHASES

Since we like to make sense of everything, let's start by thinking about life as falling into four discrete phases. (Thank you, dear friend Victoria Cressman, for first introducing us to this concept.)

PHASE 1: Your first 25 years

The dreaming years. You're sorting out who you are and who you want to be. You're forging friendships and relationships. You're going off to college. You're learning and soaking everything up.

PHASE 2: Age 25 to 45

The building years. You're putting your dreams together, slowly but surely making them come to life.

You're creating a family, navigating a career, making a home for yourself. You're busy!

PHASE 3: Age 45 to 65

The reinventing years. *What just happened? Where am I? How did I get here? Do I want to be here? What happens next?* All of a sudden, you're back where you started, with (or without) your partner. This is a time of self-assessment, evaluation, and reimagination. For some, it is pure joy to take all that we've built and our newfound confidence and rethink what we want going forward with greater perspective and a stronger inner anchor.

Phase 4: Age 65 onward

The celebrating years. This is the stage when things are looking up, up, up in terms of personal satisfaction, reduction in worry, and general happiness. Sure, your body might be a little less cooperative than you'd like, but you are enjoying your family, all that you've built, and the self-reliance you've worked so hard to create over your long life. At least, this is what we imagine it's meant to be like. We're excited to join the celebration, and who knows, perhaps cover it in our next book!

ARE WE THERE YET?

Given that you're reading this book, you're probably comfortably in Phase 2, or opening the door to Phase 3. Here's where we often feel the dissonance between where we are and where we thought we'd be. Many women go into their forties

"Fifty for me is the most joyful time. It's part of the most blissful time you'll ever have, because you circle back to the feeling of your first twenty-five years. It feels like kindergarten all over again."

Victoria, 50-ish
MILL VALLEY, CA

and fifties full of fears. *Now that I've met goals I set earlier in my life (whether it's raising kids, or achieving work milestones, or both!), what does my life mean now?* You may have believed that you'd have it all together by now, but guess what? You're still not there, wherever THERE was. Your expectation of where you would be doesn't match up to the reality.

Things your twenty-something self believed your Phase 3 self would have together:

◇ You'd have more money saved.

◇ You'd finally fully understand the difference between an FSA and an HSA.

◇ Being a mom to older kids would be SO much easier.

◇ Your closet would be perfectly curated (with only one type of hanger).

◇ You'd be a better improvisational cook (no recipe, no problem!).

◇ You'd be able to make it through a meal with your parents without acting like a teenager again.

◇ You'd have checked off at least half of the travel destinations on your bucket list.

◇ You'd be able to take a compliment with ease and grace—and definitely without shrugging it off.

◇ You'd have full fluent command of at least one foreign language.

◇ You'd have a flawless system for organizing light bulbs and batteries.

◇   You'd be able to do a yoga headstand.

◇   You'd have sorted out a skin care regimen that works for you.

◇   You'd have found your passion and purpose in life—and be immersed in it.

◇   You'd have time for yourself—finally—and know exactly how to spend it.

Who are we kidding? The truth is that only some of those things are real, and we were nuts for expecting so much of ourselves. Not to mention the fact that by setting such high expectations, we're not doing ourselves any favors, nor are we setting a good model for our children.

As a generation, we have high expectations, and we are consistently high achievers. So what has this done to our (now older) kids? While we looked at our mothers and said, "We need and want more choices, we want to achieve and be more than that," our kids are now looking at us like we're nuts, and saying, "HOW in the world am I supposed to do that??"

For some of us, our expectations were realistic. We set feasible goals, and we met them. And yet, it doesn't feel as satisfying as we thought it would be. There are two cars in the garage, you're the manager of your home and work, you have a decently good love life and a decently good body. You're precisely where you'd hoped to be, but still, that flash of fulfillment (the prize!) never comes. You did everything you'd planned; you checked all the boxes. So why doesn't it feel as good as it should? Why are you so restless, so uneasy?

THE GREATEST OF EXPECTATIONS

We can all agree that the expectations we have of ourselves are unrealistic, but where are they coming from? And why are we taking them so seriously?

Angela Tripoli is a life coach in Los Angeles who often works with women at this stage. She says the first step is to stop and ask yourself whose voice is in your head. "Women in this generation really need to ask themselves: Are they living lives based on others' expectations of them, or are they living lives around their true values? Are their expectations of themselves based on what their husband/boss/mother wants? So many women have lost any sense of balance and they're unhappy. If they're not getting back fulfillment and meaning and rejuvenation, they're empty, and that's not sustainable." The bottom line, she says, is this: "We all have to do the work of asking: What are OUR expectations for ourselves? What are OUR true values?"

In her thirties, Lydia found herself increasingly dissatisfied with her career in finance. When she was ready to go to college, her father had told her the only way he'd pay for her education was if she got a degree in economics. So that's what she did. "I wasn't strong enough to say, 'This isn't what I want.' So I went with the pattern. Now, in my forties, I'm finally doing what I want to do, as an interior designer. It took me years to figure out, but I'm finally doing something that feels like me." If your career path is based on someone else's expectations and dreams, why would you expect to be fulfilled and happy?

"On paper I had it all. The dream job—I was 'successful.' But at the core, I didn't know who I was."

Libby, 42
Honolulu, HI

Similarly, Sarah regularly wonders whether the path she's on is the one she's meant to be on. After all, it's not like she chose it. "My mom chose my career for me. She said 'You'd be a good party planner.' So I started in PR. It was fully based on her expectations for me and her assessment of what I was going to be good at. I'm still not 100 percent sure—does that tap into my most innate passions and talents? I don't know. I really wish that I would've tapped into these things when I was thirty-five."

UNHEALTHY ECHOES FROM MOMS

Many women we heard from had moms who hadn't done them any favors in setting positive expectations, or affirming the choices they made for themselves.

IS PERSONAL FULFILLMENT TOO MUCH TO ASK FOR?

Our moms rarely talked about personal fulfillment. Our husbands barely seem to understand what it means. But for us, personal fulfillment is an essential part of our being. Following our passion, feeling like the way we're spending our time is important and meaningful, is *everything*. It's just not something that's easy to articulate.

Personal fulfillment and meaning. You can think about those two terms as somewhat interchangeable. In his book *Why We Work*, Barry Schwartz argues that there is a false belief that people work primarily for pay. "While it's true we want to get paid, people are

"I'm constantly trying to envision what my future will look like— more time, less 'stuff' to take care of? All my time and experience goes to my kids. I'm a single mom. I put too much pressure on myself."

Kathy, 50
BARDSTOWN, KY

looking for work that shows you've done something worth doing at the end of the day. Meaning is the key and involves feeling that you're contributing to making someone's life better. It doesn't have to be grandiose. It can be as simple as making a small positive contribution to someone's life and feeling fulfilled because you made someone's life better."

And sometimes, isn't it enough—or maybe even everything—to make someone just feel better? As Maya Angelou famously said, "I've learned that people will forget what you said, people will forget what you did, but people will never forget how you made them feel."

If fulfillment is what we're after, it seems critical for us to make sure the goalpost is set up realistically. What might it be like to allow ourselves to feel fulfilled by the less "perfect" option? Imagine allowing yourself to be fulfilled by a good day instead of a perfect day; feeling fulfilled by a nice, tasty, enjoyable dinner instead of a dinner that could be on the cover of *Food + Wine* magazine; feeling fulfilled by making colleagues laugh so hard they cry instead of winning an award at work.

As author Jody Picoult writes, "Maybe who we are isn't so much about what we do, but rather what we're capable of when we least expect it."

THE FACEBOOK EFFECT: IS IT TIME FOR A SOCIAL MEDIA SABBATICAL?

I f we can successfully tune out the perfectionist voices in our heads, we still have to contend with the pictures on our screens. Perfectly laid tables of Martha Stewart masterpieces. Loving siblings frolicking

"My mom was a stay-at-home mom and didn't relate to me. I am the breadwinner for our family, and she feels bad for my husband. 'Oh, poor Ben, he doesn't get a home-cooked meal.' We are close, but her expectations for me were very different from what I wanted."

Shauna, 47
STUART, FL

in the sand. Sun-dappled patios with a book perfectly placed just so. A no-kids weekend away with the caption: "This man is my *everything*. Love you more today than ever." *Seriously, people?* As much as we all know those scenes are just one gem of a moment in a much more complicated day, it doesn't do much to temper our expectations of ourselves. *If she can do all that, and look like that, why can't I? What's wrong with me?*

Facebook and social media have become the modern equivalent of magazines, circa twenty years ago. Instead of seeing glossy images of strangers' homes, tables, and abs, we're seeing glossy airbrushed images of our friends' and neighbors' homes, tables, and abs. The result, though, is the same. We're left feeling inadequate, and what's worse, it's not Cindy Crawford making us feel "less than." It's some vague friend from eighth grade, who somehow seems to have it all together, leaving us to wonder, "Why isn't MY life like that?" With Cindy Crawford, at least we can pass it off as unattainable—she has a team helping her pull together that fantasy. But with that friend, well, we're in pretty similar situations, right?

If you were to take social media channels at face value, everyone else seems to have it so together. But we know by now that they aren't really telling the whole truth. Social media creates a false "perfection filter" on our lives, making it look like everyone has tidy and impossibly lovely lives.

Researchers have even started looking into the connection between social anxiety, self-esteem, and

> "Sometimes my mom will say, 'I can't believe how talented you are. I can't believe you didn't pursue more in a career.'"
>
> Kathy, 51
> NEW YORK, NY

social media. After studying hundreds of women, researchers from Ohio State University, Hope College, and Seoul National University published an article in the journal *Cyberpsychology, Behavior, and Social Networking* in 2015 titled "Hooked on Facebook: The Role of Social Anxiety and Need for Social Assurance in Problematic Use of Facebook." They observed that "there is a growing concern that excessive and uncontrolled use of Facebook not only interferes with performance at school or work but also poses threats to physical and psychological well-being." The reason? Spending too much time on Facebook can lead to feelings of jealousy and depression, and it can also increase feelings of loneliness, stress, and anxiety. In a paper published in the *Journal of Social and Clinical Psychology* in 2014, "Seeing Everyone Else's Highlight Reels: How Facebook Usage Is Linked to Depressive Symptoms," researchers looked at the psychological effect of Facebook and concluded this: "Overall results revealed that spending a great deal of time on Facebook (or viewing Facebook more frequently) is positively related to comparing one's self to others, which in turn is associated with increased depressive symptoms."

The research is consistent, and Facebook isn't the sole social media culprit. In a 2016 study entitled "Social Media Use Associated With Depression Among U.S. Young Adults," which was funded by the National Institutes of Health, researchers at the University of Pittsburgh looked deeply at the connection between the use of everything from Facebook to Pinterest to

> "If you're clinging to where you were, you can't embrace what comes next."
> **Vanessa, 40**
> PORTLAND, ME

Instagram to even LinkedIn and how people's social media usage connected with mood. Their findings? First off, we're more active than ever. People in the study used social media on average just over an hour a day and visited various accounts thirty times a week. There was a strong and consistent connection between social media use and participants' moods. Over a quarter of all participants fell into the group with elevated levels of depression. Study authors wrote that the exposure to "highly idealized representations of peers on social media elicits feelings of envy and the distorted belief that others lead happier, more successful lives."

Much like with juice cleanses or month-long drinking fasts, many women we've talked to are starting to institute social media sabbaticals in order to cleanse the mental palate and eliminate toxic psychological behaviors.

So how's this for an idea? How about if we're going to post on FB, why don't we all agree to post the crappiest, most embarrassing, most banal thing that has recently happened to us. Like maybe a picture of what our fridge actually looks like right now?

Things We'd Post on Facebook If We Were Being Really Honest

◇ "Hey guys, check out this long chin hair I just found. It literally grew in the last hour!"

◇ "Look at this god-awful meatloaf my family choked down. Counting down the days till my kids are out of the house so I don't have this dinner stress!"

#emptynesters #nomoredinnersever

◇ "Happy Anniversary, honey! Here's the latest pic of us holding hands. Sweet memories of 2001!"

◇ "How cute is our puppy Bailey? Little does my family know I love him more than them."

◇ "My dinner tonight: carrots and hummus, four glasses of wine, and five scoops of ice cream."

◇ "I'm worried I'm actually getting duller as I get older. I mean, I don't even want to hang out with me."

◇ "Hey! It's bad selfie day! Here's mine."

◇ "Don't forget to clear your browser, friends! I just winked at 4 guys on Match.com."

EXPECTATIONS THEN VS. NOW

Back when we were in Phase 1 and early Phase 2, "success" was so easy to define. Snagging that first job. Putting a pretty color of paint on the wall—ourselves! Finding a deal on a designer dress. Breaking up with a bad boyfriend and being totally okay in the end. Keeping a newborn alive and well for the first few months. Making turkey for Thanksgiving for the first time and having it turn out just fine. Check! Check! Check!

It's not like any of those things were easy, but they were clear. It was obvious what needed to be done; the boundaries were sharply defined. We knew that if we came out the other side, we would be victorious. We could feel great about ourselves.

And ultimately, being a "good mom," whatever

"I question it all the time: did I make the right decision to stay home? The idea of having it all is an extremely tough thing."

Lucy, 43
MADISON, WI

that meant, was success in and of itself. Now it's much harder to grasp what our expectations are for ourselves and what success looks like. Motherhood is CLEAR. Careers are CLEAR. This? NOT CLEAR.

In early motherhood, our kids are "ours" and we shape them. They are in essence part of our identity. Now we realize that we're merely here to guide them and let them go.

SHOULDA, COULDA, WOULDA

From what we heard in our interviews, there seems to be a lot to be afraid of at this stage of life. Regrets are a really big one. Trina, forty-eight, from Phoenix, Arizona, is pushing herself to take risks specifically to avoid having future regrets. "I have a fear of looking back and saying, 'I could've been a better mom. I wasted so much time. I should've been a doctor—or I should've been the COO of the Container Store. I don't want to look back and feel like I was lame or too afraid to go out and do something creative and cool.'"

EIGHT COMMON FEARS

◇ **Future regret**

◇ **Judgment**

◇ **Making a mistake**

◇ **Heading down the "wrong" path**

◇ **Wasting time**

◇ **Wasting money**

◇ **FOMO**—Fear of missing out on something awesome because you were too scared to take a risk

◇ **Fear of failure**

Many of us now worry about what we haven't done, and feel regretful and really find it tough to move out of this space. The feeling of "it's too late to pivot" is very real and scary, and prevents us from being open-minded to new paths. We feel judged by the choices we make or don't make—by our kids, parents, friends, neighbors, spouses.

True Confession:

"I spend so much time alone—too much."

IT'S TIME TO BE A BOSS

So here we are in midlife, overwhelmed by the reality that we won't be an opera singer, or a surgeon, or Mother Teresa. And we have residual blame of ourselves for making what we feel were the wrong choices. This regret causes us to distrust ourselves and our ability to make new choices. It's paralyzing, and it keeps us stuck.

But what if we could flip that script? What if we leveraged the knowledge, insights, and intuition we've

"Somehow, I arrived in this new place of constant change for myself, my body, my family dynamic. I am forced to adapt to what I can no longer control. I hope to God, Buddha, or Mother Nature that the skill set of adaptability I earned in mother-hood is still there, waiting to be rediscovered. It just may be the miracle that will save me from myself."

Shelly, 49
CHICAGO, IL

earned over the years and used it to really, truly make more informed, laser-focused choices—choices that are right for us?

Instead of feeling defeated, we could be looking at a huge opportunity.

THE CHOICES ARE YOURS

So much of the perfect storm makes us feel out of control. We were paralyzed by the number of choices we had to make in earlier stages of our lives *(Which school? Where do I want to live? What type of friends do I enjoy spending time with?).* Everything felt risky and wrong. We made choices all day, every day, in our work and home lives. And every little choice has been one small step on a road that has led us to where we are today. Now that we're here, we're stopped at a crossroads, faced with the chance to decide what we want next.

Here we have an opportunity. This is the moment to shift from making random choices to INTENTIONAL choices for the second half of our lives. Choices for ourselves. Choices driven by positivity instead of fear.

There can be relief in trading in our lofty responsibilities and what we think we should be doing to be successful for smaller, more tangible and meaningful moments with the people in our lives.

Where to begin? Start by writing down what it is you expect of yourself on both a day-to-day basis and on a deeper level. What are the things you expect of yourself in your relationships, with your family, and at

"I am where I thought I'd be . . . but I worked damn hard to get here."
Lynn, 52
PHOENIX, AZ

work? By writing this all down, it will allow you to challenge your own expectations and ideas.

From here, you will be able to start fresh with clear-eyed awareness of what's possible. You'll open yourself up to a vision for your future built on a foundation of open-mindedness and self-love. Imagine this: What if you were to go into midlife with expectations that it will be exciting, positive, joyful, adventurous, hopeful?

"As I get older, I try to keep things to myself. I'm afraid of judgment— 'C'mon, you haven't worked for so many years, you're so lucky!' Do people really not understand that it's a choice I've made to be a stay-at-home mom? Even my son has judgment. 'Mom, you should get a job!'

Kathy, 51
NEW YORK, NY

MIDLIFE CHECKUP: ASK YOURSELF THESE FOUR QUESTIONS:

1   What if you threw away your resume—that vision for what you thought you were? And what if you wrote a new one with a vision of what you want to do?

2   What if you exchanged what you have always pictured was success with a new, untried passion?

3   What might it look like to ditch unrealistic expectations of what your life SHOULD be, and in turn replace them with real possibilities of what your life COULD be from now on?

4   Is there something you could add to your life that would contribute to the life of someone else?

FIVE EASY STEPS TO REALIGNING EXPECTATIONS WITH (SOME SEMBLANCE OF) REALITY

1. Take a moment and think, really think, about where your expectations of yourself are coming from. Pinpoint the source: You? Your parents? Your kids? Your spouse? Your colleagues? Someone else?

2. Ask yourself: Would you expect the same of other people? It's all too common that we hold ourselves to higher standards than anyone else. And if we can't be happy with ourselves, how can we possibly be happy with others?

3. Light a candle and mourn whatever is unrealistic. (Seeing friends three nights a week and also being fresh and bright-eyed at breakfast? Maybe once a month is more achievable.) Be realistic about what's possible, and what's fulfilling for you!

4. Which of the Eight Common Fears is most profound for you? If you fear failure, set a goal for yourself to do one task you are afraid of, and give yourself a time limit to accomplish it (and the room to be bad at it for a while). Face it down so you can consciously look FORWARD, and learn to leave the regrets behind. This will positively impact your happiness (or at least clear the path for new ideas).

5. Write a new line on your life resume, all about fulfillment. What will the title and job description be to feed your inner satisfaction? Then, leave room to fill in things you want to do, but haven't done yet.

CHAPTER

4

For the First
Time, I'm
Becoming
Myself

(Finding Meaning, Community,
and Happiness)

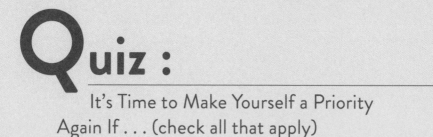

Quiz :

It's Time to Make Yourself a Priority Again If . . . (check all that apply)

- ◆ You can't remember the title of the last book you read (either it's been too long or you literally can't remember).

- ◆ The last time you went to get waxed you spent the first five minutes apologizing for the "mess" down there.

- ◆ When you find yourself with ten free minutes, your brain immediately starts to create to-do lists.

- ◆ When the tax refund arrives—and you're the first to spot it—it doesn't even occur to you to quietly treat yourself.

- ◆ Crawling into bed at 8:15 p.m. is the nicest thing you've done for yourself all day.

- ◆ You actually think that you and Meredith Grey (from *Grey's Anatomy*) could be BFFs in real life.

- You're secretly gratified when the phone rings and someone has a crisis and needs you.

- You think you might be in a permanent state of dehydration.

- Your kids have a sit-down with you to talk about your stalker-y texts to them.

- The last trip you went on was to the grocery store.

- The last "crazy party night" you had was you sipping wine while you plucked the grays out of your hair in front of the mirror.

- You made sure the dog got his annual checkup, but you're overdue for a pap smear.

n our first book, *I Was a Really Good Mom Before I Had Kids*, we asked women to prioritize everything in their lives. They shared everything from "have regular sex with my husband" to "take care of my pet." Guess what didn't make it on the list? You. Yes. That lady in the mirror. Back then, we were completely, single-mindedly, maniacally devoted to everything we could possibly think of—other than ourselves.

We're doing a little better now, but we have some work to do yet. This time around, when we asked, the answer was pretty different. We're still not ranking very high on the list, but we've made the cut, or at least we're aware that we're missing. Women's answers are now more along the lines of "I'm trying to put myself back on the list" or "I'm ready to put myself back on the list," or, at best, "I'm there, at the bottom." You're number 437, right below "order backup fridge water filter cartridges." But dammit, you're there.

Part of the issue is that we're so conditioned to think of everyone else, we're so used to jumping in on a crisis and mopping up the mess, it's almost comforting to continue along that path. In fact, it's easier to think of everyone else first, because that's become a habit. The problem is that continuing on that path, especially now that we have more time and room for ourselves, is a recipe for resentment. As another woman confessed, "Self-care has totally fallen off my radar. I know I need to snap out of it, but I just can't stop focusing on everyone else."

HAPPY, AS IN "HAPPY HAPPY"?

When we asked women if they were happy in our first book, they were perplexed by the word. Women would ask us, "Like, 'happy happy'? I'm not sure what you mean. . . ." It was legitimately hard for women with young children and crazy, busy lives to fully understand what happiness meant to them at that stage. Was it about making their kids happy? Their husband happy? Was it about finding an especially good deal on LaCroix or vino at Target? About getting over seven hours of sleep? About coming home from work and feeling at the end of the day that everything was in balance—for one perfect hour? Happiness feels like such a meaty, lofty goal. We associate it with a state of perfection, which means that it's always *just* out of reach.

◇ I can't be happy unless I've worked out so hard I've gotten rid of the underarm jiggle.

◇ I can't be happy unless everything is cleared off the counters.

◇ I can't be happy unless I'm at my goal weight (from twenty years ago).

◇ I can't be happy unless my parents, partner, and kids all recognize what I've done for them and say, "Thank you."

◇ I can't be happy unless my kids' lives are all tied up in a happy bow.

Being completely happy becomes completely impossible. Albert Camus once said, "You will never be happy if you continue to search for what happiness consists of. You will never live if you are looking for the meaning of life."

In many ways, we learned from our parents to defer gratification—and that sense of self-denial has impacted our ability to live in the moment. We are taught that validation comes with the title and/or money, so how could you possibly be happy when you don't have that next dangling carrot? What happens when we take a step back and ponder who we are and what we want?

We've made "happiness" a theoretical, academic pursuit; we're overcomplicating matters and forcing ourselves to never quite relax and embrace joy in smaller, achievable, more realistic doses.

But what if we allowed ourselves to celebrate smaller moments, to savor things that make us smile? To understand that happiness is more about enjoyment than euphoria, more about contentedness than crazy delirium, more pleasant than perfect.

The women we talked to who were truly thriving seemed to disconnect happiness from the word "success"—as if they had moved past the stigma of the word, onto a much more fluid version that involved experiencing moments, or people. They were rational and realistic about their expectations of their lives and loves. Yes, they knew their kids were amazing and beautiful miracles. But maybe, just maybe, their perfectly nice kids wouldn't necessarily discover the cure for cancer.

Meanwhile, they were more mindful of the little things that brightened their days. These were

"All I ever was valued for was my accomplishments, not for who I was. I think this is partly why our generation is filled with such perfectionists."

Rachel, 42
TRAVERSE CITY, MI

seemingly minor moments, but they brought joy all the same.

LITTLE THINGS THAT MAKE ME HAPPY NOW

◇ Volunteering at the garden center near my house

◇ The vacation I'm planning two months from now

◇ Taking a swim by myself

◇ Actually reading the book in advance of the book club meeting

◇ Spending the afternoon with a close girlfriend

◇ Sleeping in, like, for real

◇ Taking my dog for a walk, alone

NOW ON TO THE MINOR MATTER OF FIGURING MYSELF OUT

Many of us wake up in our late thirties or early forties and make it a goal to figure out "who we are." If there's one happiness crusher, figuring out "who we are" certainly qualifies. Sorting oneself out is an important goal—and one we're working on here together—but it's hard to tackle in such a theoretical and amorphous way. What does figuring yourself out actually mean? Figuring out who we are is an evolutionary process; it's something we start working on when we're kids and continue to work on until we kick the bucket. Sure, we might take brief breaks and head off course at certain stages, but we need to remember that when that happens, we

"It's never static—I find it strange when someone says, 'Oh, I'm forty and I've figured out who I am.' Who you are evolves SO much over time. It's an evolutionary process. I try to go through each stage gracefully. That's my goal. Versus having to just get to a place where I've figured it all out. That's a lot of pressure."

Gail, 49
MONTCLAIR, NJ

don't need to start all over again. We are not lost. And going slightly off course doesn't mean we don't know who we are. Instead, it simply means it's time for a little course correction.

The key is to acknowledge that we're moving through the stages of our life fluidly, that all things are connected, and we need to stay acutely aware of how we're shifting forward.

YOU FIND YOURSELF IN THE "U"

There's nothing more crazy-making than being told you're crazy. So it should come as great consolation that what we're all experiencing—this pronounced shift—is legitimate, real, and scientifically proven.

Researchers at the University of Warwick and Dartmouth College published a study in 2008, "Is Well-Being U-Shaped over the Life Cycle," showing that people's satisfaction levels follow a U-shaped curve over the course of their lives. The study authors talked to tens of thousands of people across seventy-two countries over several decades, asking, "How satisfied are you with your life overall?"

Women consistently hit their lowest point of satisfaction in their forties. The authors described the satisfaction well as a "human nadir." Said University of Warwick Economics Professor Andrew Oswald: "Some people suffer more than others, but in our data, the average effect is large. It happens to men and women, to single and married people, to rich and poor, and to those with and without children. Nobody

"I used to have LISTS AND LISTS AND LISTS, and I couldn't go to bed unless I got the items crossed off. Now I just don't care. And it's okay."

Wendy, 52
HOUSTON, TX

knows why we see this consistency. . . . However, one possibility is that individuals learn to adapt to their strengths and weaknesses, and in midlife quell their infeasible aspirations."

Barry Schwartz, author of *The Paradox of Choice,* affirms the connection between satisfaction in later stages of life and having more moderate expectations. "We have some evidence that as people age, they are more inclined to seek what's good enough instead of the best—and they are happier. A *good enough* career change is the problem that needs to be solved. It might not SOUND good enough to this generation, but it's a habit that this generation needs to break."

I KNOW WHAT DOESN'T MAKE ME HAPPY. DO I GET POINTS FOR THAT?

If some women were aware of what made them happy, several more were conscious of what they no longer associated with happiness. Women we talked to were very clear on one thing: happiness is no longer connected to tangible accomplishments they used to connect with success. And we're increasingly aware that once they met those goals they associated with "happiness," whether it was money or fame or another measure of success, it never felt quite as good or as meaningful as they had expected.

Now is the time that we all need to reassess and redefine what success actually means to each of us. Many women we talked to said that what defines success for them has shifted dramatically. It used to be about the perception or outward version of success—the tangible accomplishments. Having your job title begin with the word "Chief." Selling a boatload of houses in one week. Having your kid win the spelling bee. Even being in a long-term marriage used to be a huge goal.

HAPPINESS BY THE DECADES:

◇ In our twenties: **A job that I want to actually do. Enough money in my bank account that I can take an impulsive ski vacation. A hot hookup (and call the next morning). Having sex three times a week.**

◇ In our thirties: **A raise at work. A seriously amazing haircut. An hour to myself. A good night's sleep. Having sex three times a month.**

◇ In our forties: **Not being stressed out. Feeling productive. Feeling like my life has meaning. Feeling loved and appreciated. Feeling worthy of all of those feelings.**

Rachel, forty-nine, from Philadelphia, Pennsylvania, used to connect happiness with doing a good job at work and ascending the corporate ladder. Now, not so much. "Success isn't about what I accomplish in my career. I want to be productive, sure, but more important, I just want to do a good job RIGHT NOW. I just want to be happy and not stressed out. It's okay if it's that simple. I want short-term, attainable happiness goals. I just want to be happy RIGHT NOW. In the moment."

Dina, fifty, from Fairfax, California, is aware of how she's learning to let go of her notions of perfection

"It's important to not let how successful your kids are (or not) define you. Our generation has been taught that we've 'made' our kids successful. It's critical to see yourself as separate from your kids, not one unit."

Carolina, 41
TOPEKA, KS

in order to take more of a long view. "I get stuck in the little details about what's in front of me instead of rising up and getting the big perspective. If I can just step up and look beyond, I can let a lot of things go. They don't need to be perfect." And when she's able to step back and take an eagle's-eye view, Dina inevitably feels much calmer, happier, and more at ease with herself.

After years of pinning our sense of happiness to our children's accomplishments, many of us are now trying to sever that connection between how well *they* do and how good *we* feel. As one woman told us, "It's really tricky how intertwined our identities are in relationship to our kids' success—and the perceived connection between the two. People will say to me, 'Wow, you've done a GREAT job! Josh is such a good kid.' And if something goes sideways, we're meant to feel it's our fault, that we've worked too much, or coddled them too much. But is it our fault? We need to make sure to separate our success from our kids' success."

HOW CAN I BE HAPPY IF . . . ?

Just as it's hard for so many women to take a compliment, it is equally hard for many of us to allow ourselves to feel that happiness, calm, contentment—whatever you want to call it—is something we truly deserve. After all, there's always something that could be better, isn't there? *How can I feel happy if . . . the dog is barking/the water filter needs to be replaced/my in-laws and I disagree on*

> "For me, happiness is a blend of who you are and the person you want to be in the world; it's having some mindfulness around who I do want to be and who I don't want to be, a certain inner compass or awareness. Can I feel good about the interactions with the people I love? Not just 'I figured out this career and made a bunch of money.' What are the other paths?"
>
> Amy, 50
> AVALON, CA

politics / I haven't planned next year's Christmas vacation / there are thirteen unread emails that desperately need my attention? It could go on and on, and it does.

Angela Tripoli, a life coach in Los Angeles, says that the first step in allowing ourselves to find peace and joy is to let it be something we believe we have a right to feel. She thinks this starts with coming to terms with who you truly are. "Maybe you have to accept the fact that your values are inconsistent with your beliefs about 'what makes a good woman'? Maybe you should ask yourself this: Do I change my beliefs or stay true to my values?"

MODERN MODELS OF HAPPINESS

Finding that harmony between your beliefs and your sense of self is what Mahatma Gandhi identified as the core aspect of happiness: "Happiness is when what you think, what you say, and what you do are in harmony." There's nothing that feels better than when what we believe to be good and true is aligned with what we feel inside and how we act.

Similarly, Oprah Winfrey has spoken passionately about the connection between happiness and forgiveness. When psychiatrist Dr. Gerald G. Jampolsky appeared on her show in 1990, he shared an idea that really resonated with her and helped her see a new path to happiness. He said: "If we really want to hold on to grievances, we'll never be happy. It's really a willingness to see the person in the light of love, rather than in the action that happens." We all struggle with the act of forgiveness (even Oprah!), but once we

"I feel like I'm more interested in being ME right now than I ever was."

Virginia, 43
BEAUFORT, SC

can learn to accept that something has happened—not necessarily that it was okay, but that the moment *passed*—we can learn to forgive. And that act of forgiveness helps US feel happier.

Generosity is also something we heard from women as being an important source of happiness. And research out of the University of Oregon and published as "Neural Responses to Taxation and Voluntary Giving Reveal Motives for Charitable Donations" in *Science* magazine backs that up. Bill Harbaugh, a professor of economics at the University of Oregon, conducted a study with nineteen volunteers, each of whom got 100 dollars. He observed their brains using a functional MRI scanner, as the women either a) donated their money through a mandatory tax, b) decided to give more out of their own volition, or c) kept the money for themselves. His findings? The charitable set had the strongest brain response associated with satisfaction. Giving to others makes us happy, and in turn increases our own sense of gratification and well-being.

Sure enough, heading into the second half of our lives, the concrete acts and accomplishments we have associated with happiness and success are no longer feeling as important or so invested with meaning. And now is the perfect moment to make a choice to be happy based on different inputs.

"I feel lucky—we live in America; our kids are healthy. I have to be reminded of everything that IS working. I know I'm too hard on myself. I've had to reframe what happiness and success means."

Marci, 42
MINNEAPOLIS, MN

FINDING NEW SOURCES OF HAPPINESS

Forgiveness, generosity, and balance are only a few ways we can learn to draw out our own happiness. We heard several other inspiring ways women are building up their sense of well-being.

Making an impact

"In my twenties, success for me was about money. I was a lawyer for the money. (I really wanted to be a doctor but couldn't afford medical school.) Bottom line: I wanted money and to be successful. For me, that meant climbing the ladder. Now I realize money doesn't buy happiness. For me, what defines success is making a positive change in others' lives. That, to me, is really exciting. As a life/career coach, when I hear from women who I've helped change the direction of their careers—now that's something."

Jane, 46
LITCHFIELD, CT

PROVEN WAYS TO BUILD MORE HAPPINESS INTO YOUR DAY

Look Back: Be a rookie

Jon Rasmussen is a shaman based in Monterey, California, whom we've worked with over the years. He is the author of *Dreaming Your World into Being: The Shaman's Secrets to Having the Life You Desire Now,* and he regularly conducts retreats at Post Ranch Inn and Cavallo Point in California. Jon believes that people who consider themselves "younger" are overall

"The outward version of success that I used to pursue is gone. I no longer feel that the perception of success from other people is important. The job title, living in New York City—I don't think I need to chase that anymore. I don't need to prove anything to anyone anymore. Just myself. My passion and my joy are important, rather than keeping up with others."

Kelly, 46
JACKSONVILLE, FL

Being emotionally generous with myself and others

"One of the lessons I learned as I approached forty is to be very aware of the ME I'm bringing into the room. It's the flip side of not taking things personally. The three lessons important to me that I've learned are: One, we are all the same. Two, I need to forgive myself. And three, I need to forgive others."

Rachel, 42 TRAVERSE CITY, MI

Enjoying great relationships

"Success to me now is less about my financial and career accomplishments. Success to me now means having balance in my life and having a great relationship with my husband and my kids. Those are the things that I'm realizing are the keys to REAL success in life."

Kendra, 45 TOPEKA, KS

Staying resilient

"You look at your kids. Even through the storms we've all been through, the dysfunction, the love, the laughter, the tears, when I see them as good, caring, responsive people, that's all I can ask for. That's success to me."

Dana, 49 SONOMA, CA

Nurturing self-confidence

"I was a lot more insecure in my twenties and thirties—proving myself, defining who I was. As you get comfortable with yourself, the happiness and peace comes. For me, writing and meditation has helped with that."

Carla, 49 MACON, GA

happier. "When you get to midlife, you have a loss of adolescence and we're mourning. If we can get back to that childlike and youthful perspective, we feel lighter, joyful, more liberated; we can live in the moment."

How to get there? Start by trying something new, silly, out of your comfort zone. Anything you think of is great, as long as you are able to recall the feeling of being a true novice:

◇ **Pick up a new card game (it could be anything from Bridge to Solitaire).**

◇ **Join a chorus.**

◇ **Put on a pair of ice skates—for the first time in thirty years.**

◇ **Learn to cook.**

◇ **Plan a trip—solo.**

◇ **Learn how to speak Italian.**

◇ **Dance! Dance to loud music, in your home, and totally let go.**

Look Forward: Be mindful of what remains

Now that we're in the second half of our lives, that means that we have about half of a certain number of experiences left—or half as many *still left* to experience (the glass is half full, not half empty!). It can be powerful to actually quantify (as much as that's possible) just how many amazing experiences still remain for us. Sonja Lyubomirsky of the University

"I am where I thought I'd be at this point in my life. And part of me is disappointed."

Caroline, 48
SOUTHFIELD, MI

of California, Riverside, copublished an article, "Pursuing Happiness: The Architecture of Sustainable Change," in the *Review of General Psychology*. In this study, she and her coauthors found that just about half of what accounts for our happiness levels is based on choices we make. Life circumstances (marriage, money, kids) play some part, but they only account for about 10 percent of our happiness. Meanwhile, our attitudes around our lives—whom we choose to spend our time with, what we choose to do, and how we look at the world we live in—are instrumental in increasing our happiness. That's why paying attention to what remains instead of what has already passed is one way we can be more mindful—and joyful—in those moments.

Think about how many of these experiences are left. By being mindful of them in advance, you may just enjoy the next one (and the one after it) even more:

◇ Summers

◇ Vacations

◇ Sunrises

◇ Full moons

◇ Ski seasons

◇ Girlfriend getaways

◇ Fourth of July block parties

◇ Halloween costumes

◇ Season finales of the latest HBO addiction

"All my life I've been the nice girl: let's get along, let's do what we're supposed to do at work. It's not working for me anymore. For the first time in my life, I have a disruptor mentality—I'm not a pleaser anymore. Instead of being the person who impresses others, for the first time, I'm passionate about what I'm doing and I'm really ready to disrupt and do stuff that makes other people uncomfortable."

Jane, 46
LITCHFIELD, CT

Look Inside: Get comfortable saying no

As we're rediscovering our inner child and savoring our future moments, it's also critical to get clear about our priorities, which are different now. And saying "no" is key to staying true to those priorities. Warren Buffett once said that "the difference between successful people and really successful people is that really successful people say no to almost everything." That measure of success holds just as true in life and relationships as it does in business. Dr. Kathlyn Hendricks believes learning to say no is foundational to hearing our own inner voices. As she told us: "We need to make choices that come from what is really authentic and sustainable, rather than trying to adapt and react to a culture and the demands that can't be met."

THINGS WE ALL HAVE PERMISSION TO SAY **NO** TO NOW:

◇ Dinner parties with couples you enjoy only 50 percent of. (How about just spending time with the one you actually like?)

◇ Eating a meal you don't like. No more time for things that are not completely delicious.

◇ Command performances with in-laws. You are old now too. You get to be cranky sometimes.

◇ Feeling bad when a frenemy says something that weirdly festers in your brain. No more frenemies in this life from now on.

Things to Say YES to Now:

◇ That girls' trip

◇ That solo trip

◇ The concert you've always wanted to see

◇ Getting that second dog

◇ That extra glass of wine

◇ Enrolling in that cooking class

◇ A quickie in a public restroom

◇ Dating again

◇　Working on the weekends when it's not something that will actually make a big difference.

◇　That movie. That charity event. That school thing.

◇　Taking care of your neighbor's ridiculously yippy Chihuahua (again).

SEVEN EASY WAYS TO MAKE HAPPINESS A PRIORITY

1. Ask yourself if "happy" applies to you or is a goal. Consider "relevance" or "finding meaning."

2. Allow yourself to be comfortable—really, truly comfortable—with the idea that you DESERVE happiness.

3. If you are feeling blocked from being happy, consider what is standing in your way. Is it something you have control over? Are your expectations of what could make you happy realistic in your life?

4. Think about what used to make you happy, and the moments in the past where you've felt pure joy. What was at the heart of those experiences? Family bonding? Self-acceptance? Childlike wonder? Relaxation?

5. Make happiness—or whatever word replaces it for you—a choice. For some women, happiness is a static state. For others, it seems to be an active choice. Happiness can be a powerful decision that you make—for yourself—and that you and only you can deliver on.

6. Identify five mini happy moments you can acknowledge in your day. What are things that bring you joy? When they happen, be aware and sit with that feeling.

7. Consider JOY a goal, versus happiness. And when you encounter that feeling, write it down, so you build an index to remind you what truly brings you joy.

CHAPTER

5

Do These Crow's Feet Make My Ass Look Big?

(Redefining the Idea
of Beauty)

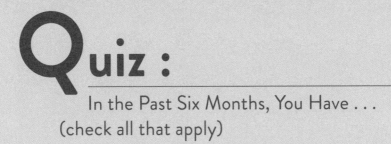

Quiz :

In the Past Six Months, You Have . . .
(check all that apply)

- Stood in front of the mirror and tugged at your cheeks/eyes/neck/ears/perimeter of nose.

- Lied to a friend about having had an injection. Fessed up. Recommended dermatologist to friend.

- Complained about looking *so tired*.

- Magnified a picture of a celebrity online to see what traces of freckles, spots, and grooves you could find in her face. Felt momentarily better about self.

- Completely committed to a new fitness regimen. Quit new fitness regimen after three (interminable) weeks.

- Finally purged closet of pants that induce state of despair (how did these *ever* fit?).

- Looked at your debit card receipts and realized in horror how much money it costs for the upkeep of a middle-aged woman.

- Proudly/loudly/defiantly shared age with group of younger women.

- Dodged question of age with group of younger women.

- Felt sexier than ever before.

- Walked by a group of men sitting on a curb and silently willed them to objectify you. #nodice

- Been *shocked* by the disconnect between what you thought you looked like and the image looking back at you in a mirror.

- Realized your *teeth* are looking old. Is it time for braces, again?

- Raided your teenage daughter's makeup case for "on-trend" lip gloss colors.

- You look in the mirror and can't help but compare yourself to what you looked like 10 years ago.

The most confusing thing right now is how conflicted we all feel about our looks. Our bodies are morphing and changing shape, and yet, we're somehow feeling newly confident in our sagging skin. How weird is that?!

Our hands are shriveling, our underarms are jiggling, our skin is drooping, and perhaps worst of all, no one is paying any damn attention to us. Perhaps the biggest awkward confession of all in our lives is just how much we care about how we look. Of course, we're smart enough to realize the implicit hypocrisy in this. Worrying about our vanity goes against our value systems—there's so much else we know we should be thinking about. And as mothers, the last thing we want to do is make our daughters believe looks define who we are. But the aging anxieties are legitimate, and the wrinkles are only getting deeper. So before we can dig into the meatier stuff of this book, the stuff of our hearts and souls, we have to just buff the outer layer.

The truth of the matter is that all of a sudden this aging s*%$ has gotten real and our bodies are giving us away. There is definitely a not-so-small part of us that kinda believes life might be a bit better if we had the perfect ass.

What's ironic about this is that in so many ways, we've never felt more at home in our bodies, more confident and proud. We have complicated relationships with all of our scars and wrinkles and freckles. On the one hand, the growing list of imperfections is a visible sign of wear and tear that shows our age. But on the flip side, we've come this far, earned every wrinkle, and have many more ahead of us. Every freckle is a reminder of a summer beach day. Every wrinkle is a hilarious laugh with a girlfriend. A stretch mark is a kid—thank you very much. These are moments we're proud of, events we wouldn't want to take back. The problem is, as much as we'd like to remind ourselves of all that, we still have to admit that we covet the smooth foreheads, plump lips, perky boobs, and bright eyes we see on women on TV, in magazines, and in our own photos from ten years back.

WHY IS NO ONE LEERING AT ME ANYMORE?

It's kind of a twisted situation. In our twenties, when we're supposedly the best looking of our lives, our self-esteem is so low. We don't know what we have. Many women, when they were younger, built their identities based around the perception of them—how others defined what "beauty" or "attractiveness" looked like, and how they fit into that picture. We were so busy trying to figure ourselves out and fit in that we were unable to be and love ourselves.

Now, the situation is flipped. We have (for the most part) accepted our flaws and learned to love our bodily quirks. We have our own definition of attractiveness, and we're primed and ready to prance down the street in full glory.

If only anyone would look.

All of a sudden we are *invisible*. This was something we heard over and over from women.

As our bodies and faces shift, sometimes dramatically, we are seen differently from the outside world, and this transition can be painful for many women. In the TV show *Younger*, one character says, "One day you're beautiful and then BAM! You have an 'age spurt' and you're OLD!"

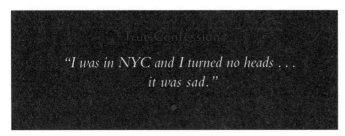

True Confessions

"I was in NYC and I turned no heads . . . it was sad."

I Lie About My . . .

While some of us are completely accepting and proud of our imperfections, let's just be honest, we're all lying about *something*. Here are some confessions of what some of us lie about:

◇ **Age (the number one thing we lie about)**

◇ **Weight**

◇ **Height**

◇ **State of my marriage**

◇ **Wine intake**

◇ **Being SOOOO busy**

◇ **Frequency of working out**

◇ **Hair color**

◇ **Botox addiction**

◇ **Kids' ages**

"I look at pics of myself as a teen. If I could have one thing now that would be different— it's that fresh skin, and I would appreciate it!!"

Cherie, 42
ALDORA, GA

At the same time, we're stronger in so many ways, and if we embody that confidence, we can be sexier than ever. That's a seductive and powerful thing—and we have the choice and capability and experience to feel this way *now*—so much more so than we did at twenty. In an interview with *InStyle* for the February 2017 issue, an A List celebrity talked about how she experiences this new self-confidence as a revelation (yes, even she can feel bad about herself). "When I turned forty, I felt like I got this free software upgrade that I wasn't expecting," she told the magazine. "It just happened. Suddenly I was like, 'Oh, this is fantastic: I don't care! I like myself, and I'm just going to live my life. I'm going to stop worrying and tearing myself down.'"

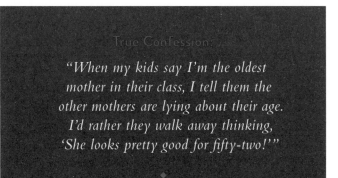

True Confession:

"When my kids say I'm the oldest mother in their class, I tell them the other mothers are lying about their age. I'd rather they walk away thinking, 'She looks pretty good for fifty-two!'"

WHO DO THESE LEGS BELONG TO!?

It would be nice if we all felt that way all the time, but the truth is, many of us find this aging business so distressing—in large part because we stop recognizing ourselves as our bodies change shape. We look

FACE: "As I look in the mirror I try to pull back these jowls that were *not* there last year!!"
Candice, 49 CHELSEA, SD

ARMS: "If I put my arm out, I'm like 'why do I have a *flap*—like my arm isn't on my arm? It's hanging off my bone!' It's not that I'm that vain. But it's an out-of-body experience. What happened to this body? It's easy to forget that we're part of nature and this is what happens—it's the circle of life. Yet it's hard to remember all that in the moment. This shit will send me into a *state*."
Samantha, 47 OAKLAND, CA

HANDS: "No one told me I would get cellulite from my elbows to my ankles. It would be great to hear that—seriously, what happened to my thighs?? When did my hands become shriveled up?
Tawna, 43 MIAMI, FL

ELBOWS: "Yeah the fat around my elbows—I'm sitting here doing a plank and there's this fat around my elbows and there's *no* workout for that!!"
Sarah, 52 STUDIO CITY, CA

BELLY: "For me, it's the muffin top! That thing that hangs over your jeans. Do I have to tuck in my shirt a new way now? It's all about camouflage! If I'd had a C-section—and had that scar already—I would probably get that pooch taken care of. Ten years from now, maybe there will be a miracle cure for the pinchable area! In the meantime, I just have to sit up straighter to compensate!"
Kerry, 52 MEQUON, WI

BIKINI AREA: "What do you do about the hair down there that you can no longer laser?? That's disgusting!! I look down and I'm like OMG—it's awful!! It's getting less dense down there—it's atrocious!"
Rosa, 39 CORAL GABLES, FL

KNEES: "Sagging skin is my biggest nemesis! When did I get my grandmother's knees?"
Tawna, 43 MIAMI, FL

LEGS: "The physical part is *really* surprising to me. My feet were beautiful and perfect—shoot, my legs were beautiful and perfect. After I turned forty-five things started breaking. I had a plantar fascia rupture. Then I was wearing the wrong shoes walking the dog and I developed an inflamed nerve—and I'm like, 'All right, how do I fix this?' I had to have an operation!"
Layla, 46 SOUTHFIELD, MI

FEET: "I had a panic attack the other day. I look down at my hands or my neck or my *feet* and I'm thinking, 'Whose feet are these?' These look so different from how I feel on the inside. I'm not sure whose body I'm walking around in and it's a weird feeling."
Brie, 43 PORTLAND, OR

in the mirror, we look down at our legs, and we see our moms, or even worse, our grandmothers. Many of us experience this as a powerful form of grief and loss, an unwelcome shifting of our identity. As one woman put it, "There's a fundamental change happening with my body, my wrinkles. You can't deny gravity. It's there. It's real." From head to toe, we heard women struggling with all aspects of their shape-shifting. Call it the midlife version of that obnoxiously annoying kids' song "Head, Shoulders, Knees, and Toes."

True Confession

"It's taking me a little more confidence to wear the sexy stuff. Now I'm like, 'Okay . . . here I go . . . jumping into cold water to put a sexy dress on.'"

In an article in *Vogue*'s January 2017 issue about her foray into non-invasive treatments, the newly fifty Jancee Dunn writes about ways her body has shifted. "Gravity finds us all, no matter how many green drinks you tip back or how diligently you hit the gym. One of the many consequences of what I'll call middle-age resting face is that I'll look irritated when I'm in a perfectly sunny mood. Research has found that older faces are often rated as appearing more negative, presumably because of age-related changes. I'm constantly reassuring my young daughter that nothing's wrong—I just have a permanent frown."

"We're all gonna get old and get wrinkles. I say whatever you can do, do it and don't feel bad. I find that makeup is SUPER important— try going to Nordstrom and getting your makeup done properly, and you'll look in the mirror and think, 'Okay, I feel good.' That is half the battle."

Kerry, 52
MEQUON, WI

I WORK ON MYSELF, AND I'M PROUD OF IT

As we play out this new game of Head, Shoulders, Knees, and Toes (2.0), there are any number of services at the ready to help trim, tighten, or just temporarily camouflage. As one woman told us, "We have the tools to keep ourselves young; give me those injections and I'll keep using them as long as I can." Our moms had the potential to have tummy tucks and face lifts; we have everything from Botox to Ultherapy.

> True Confession:
>
> *"I keep taking the best naked selfies I can and locking them away in a hidden folder on my phone so when I'm seventy I can swoon over them."*

Beyond the options available to us, one thing that's notably different about our generation is that while our moms, if they had work done, did their best to pretend they didn't, so many more of us are unabashedly proud of our aesthetic self-improvement. Wherever you fall on the spectrum, from monthly facials to fillers, these days we trade doctors' contact info instead of nanny recommendations, real estate agents, and recipes. For many of us, the self-care has become a necessary part of life, an ever-increasing list of appointments that need to be made. It's much more about personal maintenance than pampering—and we're *not* apologizing about it.

Oh, c'mon, stop now! . . . Compliments we all love

◇ You're not old enough to have kids that age!

◇ You look thirty-five!

◇ Your *skin* looks so beautiful!

◇ You look radiant!

◇ You look so well rested.

◇ You look happy.

◇ You're hot!

◇ You're sexy!

◇ What's your workout routine?

◇ Tell me what cleanse you just did—you're glowing!

◇ Your arms are so defined.

◇ You've got so much energy.

"I never used to take care of myself. Now the maintenance is *annoying*! It's not even pampering anymore—this is a necessity! Hair alone is something I have to deal with once a month. That's two hours of my life I can't get back to cover the grays!"

Cynthia, 55
SANTA FE, NM

HEALTHY INSIDE AND OUT

I t's not just how we look that we are trying to work on; it's also how we feel on the inside. If we even have some semblance of our mothers' midlife crisis, it manifests in the way we think about getting and staying in shape.

It's tough to think about, no doubt, but we're increasingly aware of the wide array of benefits of staying fit. Not that anyone is saying it's easy! Our metabolisms significantly slow down—by as much as 25 percent, believe it or not—in our forties, which is basically like saying you have to work harder but eat less. How much less? Think about it in terms of a whole meal a day.

It's been proven time and time again that thirty minutes of activity per day has profound positive effects on everything from stress reduction to blood pressure to, yes, weight loss. But perhaps most important at this stage, exercise is just so good for our brains.

Getting the recommended thirty minutes of exercise five days a week has been proven to:

◇ **Grow specific regions of the brain related to memory**

◇ **Preserve brain tissue**

◇ **Create more new brain cells**

In a prominent study conducted out of Washington University in St. Louis and published in 2012 in the *Archives of Neurology*, scientists found a clear connection between regular exercise and the potential to ward off Alzheimer's. Volunteers who exercised at levels recommended by the American Heart Association were able to lower their levels of a protein that is a marker for the death of important neurons. As one of the study authors, Denise Head, told the *New York Times*: "The good news is that we found that activity levels, which are potentially modifiable, could have an impact, on plaque accumulation—and presumably on the course of Alzheimer's—in people with a genetic predisposition to the condition."

Another study, published in the journal *Lancet Neurology* in 2014, went on to actually quantify the impact of exercise on Alzheimer's and dementia. Getting in three twenty-minute bursts of vigorous exercise per week, such as jogging or soccer, or five thirty-minute sessions of moderate activity, such as walking, cut participants' risk of developing dementia by 82 percent.

Generationally it's a new idea that being active and healthy is now the norm, and that we need to stay active for the rest of our lives. Up until now, we may have thought about exercise in terms of vanity. But at this age, it's no longer about how we look—it's about keeping ourselves fit and strong. It's our responsibility to do all that so we can live longer and be healthier for our spouses, our kids, even our aging parents.

"I just want my kids to be proud of me—they saw me go from the couch to running a marathon (and back to the couch). This is what you can do in midlife—this is what you can achieve. I'm all about proving it to my kids."

Kelly, 46
JACKSONVILLE, FL

WHO CAN WE BLAME?

If only we could all experience a fortieth-year software upgrade that mutes our inner and outer critics. But the truth is that so many of us feel judgment, coming from every which way—including from within. It's not like society and the media are helping set positive visual examples for what we are supposed to look like!

Our expectations of what we should look and act like are so incredibly high. It's no wonder so many women find themselves with teetering self-esteem and wavering confidence both personally and professionally. Dr. Jill Muir-Sukenick, a psychoanalytic psychotherapist and one of the authors of *Face It: What Women Really Feel as Their Looks Change and What to Do about It*, says in her book that our youth-oriented culture tends to pathologize aging as if it were a disease. As a result, women get identity crises as they get older.

Part of the problem is that we don't have troves of women to look to as models. Case in point: 62 percent of the female population in the United States is over forty, but older men appear ten times more often in the media as women the same age. Things are changing slowly—the last Bond girl was over fifty—but not as quickly as we would like.

The absence of positive visual role models only feeds into our own self-criticism, says Dr. Kathlyn Hendricks, the coauthor (with her husband) of *Conscious Loving* and a regular guest on *Oprah*. "I've met thousands of women, and there are only TWO that

"What does a fifty-year-old look like? The only model [over fifty] is Christie Brinkley—and that is just a big, fat, f*cking lie, whatever is going on there."

Samantha, 48
PORTLAND, OR

loved their bodies. I've worked with famous women, gorgeous women—it doesn't matter. The way the culture works is that you're never gorgeous enough! Or there's always someone in the culture that is more gorgeous, creating a competitiveness. All of this keeps women separated from each other."

It doesn't help that the older male models often proudly show their wear and tear, while the female models the same age are often stretched and Botoxed within an inch of their lives. A man with deep creased smile lines and salt-and-pepper hair is sexy. And if he's fit with a full head of gray hair—now that qualifies him as a *silver fox*. (Note: there is *no* female complement equivalent to silver fox. . . .)

It's interesting to consider that one reason men may age with more acceptance is that they're either willfully oblivious to or utterly forgiving of their flaws. Either way, they tend to wear their gray well.

Our society's natural obsession with youth culture tends to make us give up on ourselves prematurely. As the women we revere fade out of sight, we fear we'll disappear, become irrelevant, or lose our options and opportunities. This is especially an issue for women who have relied on their looks to fuel their paths and identities. When our appearance isn't in sync with how we feel we should look, it can negatively affect our confidence—and we embody that negative perception. It's truly rare to find any woman of middle age who hasn't been affected by society's perception of females over forty.

"It's such a double standard. Why can men go gray and it's considered sexy, yet we're fighting it like mad?"
Keira, 39
CHARLESTON, SC

"Would my life be that much better if I had the perfect ass? I'm all for doing a little something to look better—but it really has to come from the inside."
Marsha, 47
SCOTTSDALE, AZ

Women our age we think are beautiful for their wit, humor, philanthropy, and overall incredible talent (in no particular order):

◇ **Michelle Obama**

◇ **Ellen DeGeneres**

◇ **Meryl Streep**

◇ **Ruth Bader Ginsberg**

◇ **Joan Didion**

◇ **Anna Wintour**

◇ **Oprah Winfrey**

◇ **Julianne Moore**

◇ **Viola Davis**

◇ **Amy Tan**

◇ **Gloria Steinem**

◇ **Jill Kargman**

◇ **Christy Turlington**

◇ **Sheryl Sandberg**

◇ **Emma Thompson**

◇ **Elizabeth Warren**

◇ **Cate Blanchett**

◇ **Salma Hayek**

◇ **Jessica Alba**

"I'm all about moving forward now. Do I wish I was twenty-one again? Of course! But then I'd miss out on all the good stuff happening now!"

Valerie, 55
SAN FRANCISCO, CA

REFRAMING AND RECLAIMING OUR OWN BEAUTY

As with so many other matters of midlife, this is an opportunity for us to shift our mindset. If we were able to look at midlife as not about losing but about transitioning, blossoming, and perhaps even getting *better*, we might be able to remove some of the societal stigma. We love what one woman told us: "The key I've found is to not resist midlife. Before I was trying to break it like a rock."

We have such a clear—and unappealing—picture of what "midlife" is supposed to look like, what we are supposed to feel, and even how we are meant to deteriorate. The generations before us have passed on their wisdom about how we're supposed to experience this phase, emotionally and physically.

But so what?

We are ready to do it differently, to reframe the conversation and put a different filter on our perspective of ourselves. We have a unique way to embrace this new chapter with a new mindset, a new way of looking at living.

It all starts with accepting and redefining what beauty means to us, reframing our attitudes about ourselves, becoming more generous, and seeing everything we've done as a worthy and beautiful part of our personal narrative.

"I hope we are reinventing fifty for our kids. The sheer virtue of how old I am with young kids—there is a part of me that keeps me younger."

Beth, 49
KATY, TX

Questions to consider:

◇ What if you thought of aging as an opportunity instead of a problem?

◇ What would it look like if you thought of aging as an experience?

◇ Could you reframe your "flaws" in a new way (i.e., those stretch marks = wonderful children)

◇ What would it mean to you to "disrupt" your own aging?

◇ Could you imagine "experience" being the new youth currency?

◇ What if our society applauded and rewarded battle scars?

At this stage in our lives, we've accumulated many valuable assets that our younger counterparts lack: wisdom, experience, time-tested strategies, learned lessons, awareness, capacity for love, the ability to recover. We have the power to leverage so much information and knowledge and insight—all of which we can use to help empower ourselves to stay healthy, stay fit, and stay confident.

THE POWER OF SELF-IMAGE AND A POSITIVE MINDSET

This change in mindset is not just a surface fix; there's real science backing up the connection between our self-perception and our health and well-being. Dr. Ellen J. Langer is a professor of

"I used to hate being invisible— now I consider it my superpower."

Rena, 51
DETROIT, MI

"I really don't have any full-length mirrors in my house; all I have is a tilted skinny mirror—I look at the part of the reflection that I like!"

Amy, 50
AVALON, CA

psychology at Harvard and the author of *Counter Clockwise: Mindful Health and the Power of Possibility*. In 2010, she conducted a study where she gave women "makeovers"—fixing up their hair and makeup and more. She took their blood pressure before and after. Guess what? Post-makeover, the women in her study had measurable decreases in their blood pressure.

Any ounce of increased confidence we experience is a self-perpetuating gift. It's been proven that even *acting* confident is perceived to be more attractive than having traditionally good looks. In a study conducted by Dr. Monica Moore out of Webster University in St. Louis, making strong eye contact and smiling—both markers of confidence—made people more attractive in the eyes of others.

Whether projecting out confidence or holding on, inside, to a more youthful self-image, it's possible that your mindset and actions can translate into a good look for you. And while Langer's work involved looks, that's not always necessary to reap the rewards. Some women are making very conscious choices to not alter their faces or bodies in any way—call it an "anti-needle" mentality. Not that they don't care about their appearance. Most of the women we know in this camp tend to take care of themselves, mind, body, and spirit. It shows via the twinkle in their eyes that inspires everyone around them. They feel confident with who they are now, and they feel centered and calm and have a childlike wonder about the exciting things around the corner. They really know what nourishes them both mentally and physically, and they're an

"Whatever with the wrinkles—it doesn't matter. I worry about not being relevant . . . not having a full life."

Virginia, 49
BEAUFORT, SC

"I used to always think, 'Fifty is *old*!' And then somebody told me, 'Old is ten years older than your age.'"
Deirdre, 49 STAMFORD, CT

"When I was younger I thought being forty and fifty was *so old.* My mom was a housewife. She looked older and didn't do things like I do now, and she didn't feel like how I feel now. In that sense, I don't feel like I'm in my fifties."
Jan, 52 ROCKLAND, ME

"We strive for perfection. We're so driven to hold on to that youth. And it only gets harder! But we should take it easier on ourselves and not expect such perfection. Look at Meryl Streep—she's not the perfect flawless woman. She's a strong independent woman who doesn't force it. I don't want to be defined by what other people think—do they think I'm pretty? I'm not going to let other people define who I am. I'll decide that for myself."
Jane, 46 LITCHFIELD, CT

"Appreciate your age because in ten years you will wish you were back there."
Doryn, 49 STAMFORD, CT

inspiration to everyone around them, including us! So many women look better now because they know themselves and their bodies, and they feel confident in a way they didn't before.

They show us how it's possible to make conscious choices about what makes you feel beautiful—you feel stronger, better, healthier, and empowered. Just look at Alicia Keys, who in addition to being an incredible singer, is perhaps most known now for going without makeup (imagine that!?). You might not be skinny or have perfect skin or a taut neck or wrinkle-free knees, or . . . or . . . or . . . But feeling good from the inside out and putting that confidence into the world is a whole different kind of beauty—and it's contagious.

WHAT MAKES US FEEL BEAUTIFUL?

When we asked women, "What makes you feel the most beautiful?" we got some insightful answers. Hearing their sentiments made it so clear that it's critically important to give ourselves permission to do the things that make us feel beautiful on a regular basis. What if we gave ourselves permission to strive to feel the *most* beautiful we ever have in our lives, right now?

I feel most beautiful when . . .

◊ "I'm post-workout"

◊ "I'm being true to myself"

◊ "I'm listening to my body and eating healthy foods without being a freak about it"

"I'm like two twenty-year-olds—but better."
Victoria, 41
WINDSOR, VT

"I surround myself with good friends who make me feel good about myself. I have the privilege to be around amazing women."
Phyllis, 49
ALBION, MI

- ◇ "I'm doing yoga"

- ◇ "I take care of myself without obsessing about it"

- ◇ "I give myself permission to feel special"

- ◇ "I pay a compliment to a stranger and make them smile back"

- ◇ "I'm laughing hysterically"

- ◇ "I'm connecting to the people in my life who really get me"

- ◇ "I'm treating myself with kindness and compassion"

- ◇ "I'm imparting well-earned wisdom to help another woman"

Now ask yourself: What makes *you* feel the most beautiful?

"Part of me is like, 'I'm okay with *now* being curvier and bigger and happier in my skin. I don't feel like I need to be a certain size. I'm not into the Botox thing; as long as I age gracefully I'll be fine. I don't want to be overdone.'"

Evelyn, 43
CARSON CITY, NV

"I've always felt sexy! Even sexier now. Would I like to have my twenty-year-old skin back? YES! If that's the worst thing that's gonna happen to me—not looking so youthful—then that's pretty good."

Cherie, 45
BALTIMORE, MD

"Getting compliments about how I look is *fine*, but it doesn't sustain me. It doesn't get me through the tough times. Having incredible, genuine friends who support me—that feeds me."

Jennifer, 53
AUBURN, IL

SIX SIMPLE STEPS TO FINDING YOUR INNER (AND OUTER) BEAUTY

1. Think back to the last time you felt gorgeous. What were all of the elements of the experience? Try to make room in your life—on a regular basis—to make even one of those actions more consistent.

2. Meditate! Even ten minutes a day of slowing yourself down, breathing deeply, and practicing mindfulness can help bring out your inner glow (and it's been proven to make you look and feel more youthful!).

3. Take a look at yourself in the mirror with an eye to the features you *love*. Maybe some days it'll just be your nail polish color or the length of your torso, and that's awesome.

4. Befriend someone twenty years older whom you admire. Absorb what makes her glow.

5. Write yourself a note about all that you love, physically. Put it in an envelope, stash it away, and pull it back out when you find yourself in a physical funk. Better yet, snap a selfie NOW, and in ten years you'll look back and think, "Holy smokes, that chick is hot!"

6. Give yourself a pass to do what feels good. Get Botox, don't get Botox—but whatever you do, forgive yourself, enjoy, and move on!

CHAPTER

5a

SPECIAL
SECTION

(Menopause Made
Me Do It)

After fully writing this book, we realized that no book on this topic could possibly be complete without dealing with the other "M" word. Not money, not marriage therapy. Yes, yes . . . menopause. So turn the page if. . .

◇ You're sort of kind of intrigued by WTF the definition actually IS, when it starts, and what to do when it happens.

◇ You are grossed out by the word "menopause" itself.

◇ You're having some weird symptoms and wonder if you're nuts or actually hormonally challenged. (You might be both. Just saying.)

◇ You now have a compulsive need to turn the page, just because we warned you that something taboo is behind it.

◇ You're ready to reclaim yourself at this time, starting with understanding what in the hell is happening.

Of course, we could write a whole book on menopause. But after bringing up the subject with a whole bunch of women—and dipping our own toes in these very waters—we've been struck by a few things that speak to the need to clear things up in the simplest possible way. First, a few observations:

1 Almost everyone cringes when you talk about menopause. The topic, the word, even the thought makes people say YUCK. Even those of us living it can barely talk about it.

2 We are not clear on when it starts and what it entails.

3   Our doctors have largely disappointed us, by either denying that what we're experiencing is real, or by trying to ply us with hormones (and not enough information) to make us go away.

4   There are actually some amazing positives that people tend to not focus on, starting with not having to being a slave to your monthly period. . . .

"No one talks about it! It's untapped territory. I haven't had any symptoms yet, but from what I've heard it sounds AWFUL! I don't know what I'm supposed to do or expect. Night sweats—is that it? It's a dirty, dark secret that people don't want to talk about. Where are the doctors? And why is no one talking about it??"

Trista, 45
DETROIT, MI

Considering that this is arguably the biggest transition of our lives, physically and mentally, it's pretty shocking that it is all so totally taboo. We've heard many stories from women about being fearful of what to expect, being super confused about whether they're in it yet or not (and what to do about symptoms), and not being able to talk with anyone about it (including their doctors, who often shrug the topic off!) and craving answers to their questions. We actually considered hiding this chapter, because it's traditionally such an uncomfortable topic, but ultimately we decided to make it more of a special bonus chapter. Freed from periods, we are reclaiming ourselves, not losing ourselves. This is natural, this is big, this is freeing, and this is happening to all of us. As one woman asked us, "How can we life-hack menopause if we're not even talking about it?"

The fact that doctors are disappointing us is the biggest surprise of all—though even in the health community, they readily acknowledge their shortfalls. In fact, in an article published in Kaiser's *Permanente Journal* called "Management of Menopause and Midlife Health Issues: What Do Midlife Women Want from Primary Care Clinicians?" it was found that of 665 women in a survey, more than half left their medical appointments with unanswered questions about menopause and hormone therapy. In the article, the authors stated, "women want to learn about menopause and their health care options but are not receiving the information and consultation they need."

It feels strange to suddenly be thrown into this "old person's" territory. Yet it's a natural process that affects each and every one of us. We can actually get ahead of it, and not be so tortured by our transitions, if only we can wrap our brains around the facts. So that's what we're here to do. In this special section, we will:

◇ Outline the basics of what to expect when you're . . . expecting

◇ Demystify the topic by sharing other women's experiences

◇ Set the record straight by uncovering what's happening to us, dry vaginas and all

◇ Lift the veil of secrecy and do whatever we can to shut down any shame

"I talk about it daily, but a lot of women our age aren't in it yet. In this day and age, we shouldn't have to FIGURE IT OUT. Even my daughter will say, 'Oh, Mommy, you're having a flash!'"

Shauna, 47
STUART, FL

True Confession:

"I just missed my first period. I'm freaking out! Will my vagina dry up next Wednesday??"

We're not going to pretend we're doctors (though we did talk to some good ones!). What are we? Great listeners and connectors. And what we heard was that women are hungry for real information from each other, confirmation that what we're feeling is normal, and a community to turn to for solace and sometimes maybe even a laugh.

So consider this a beginner's guide to try and just open up the topic and get you started—so that you can talk with your doctor, friends, mom, kids, and perhaps even a partner (eh, okay, maybe, maybe not).

FIRST OFF, LET'S SHARE SOME FACTS:

There are a lot of us here!

There are currently 123 million women between the ages of forty and sixty-five, and in the United States, there are 65 million menopausal women.

Perimenopause is a *thing*, and it can start in our forties

We hear a lot of talk of menopause, but there's actually a pre-game to the fun. And it's not entirely all that different from the main act. Here are a few things to know about perimenopause:

◇ **It can last anywhere from four to eight years. Yes, that long!**

◇ **The first signs are inconsistent periods (but it's worth noting, YOU CAN STILL GET PREGNANT!).**

◇ **In our forties, we're still producing estrogen and progesterone.**

"I call it a going-out-of-business sale. It's completely drastic markdowns and it's awful. I have to wake up in the middle of the night to change my pad!"

Dawn, 48
CHICAGO, IL

- Many of the symptoms exactly mirror menopause, which can be confusing.

- Women in perimenopause are not good candidates for hormone therapy.

- You might consider low-dose birth control pills for relief of symptoms.

The average age for the full-on show is fifty-one

Everyone is different, but the average age for women to reach menopause is fifty-one—that said, some women start as early as the mid-forties, and some arrive by their late fifties.

- The formal marker of transitioning from perimenopause to menopause is the absence of a period for twelve months.

- Your ovaries stop producing estrogen or progesterone.

- You are a candidate for estrogen therapy.

So, what do perimenopause and menopause actually look like, sound like, and feel like? Of course, the experience is different for everyone, but these are some common symptoms.

It's physical

No, it's not just hot out.

- Hot flashes

- Sleeplessness

- Weight gain

"To me the hardest thing is people trying to put me in a box that I don't want to be in. I want to know that we're not all alone, and as women we're going through different things at different times all together. But I don't want to hear, 'You're DOOMED. Here comes MENOPAUSE!'"

Casey, 47
LIVONIA, MI

- ◇ Fatigue
- ◇ Skipped periods
- ◇ Urinary changes
- ◇ Vaginal dryness (eww, but there are ways to deal) and therefore: painful sex
- ◇ Decreased sexual drive
- ◇ Accelerated loss of eyesight and hearing
- ◇ Graying pubic hair (sorry, we heard a lot about this one, so we thought we should include it)

It's emotional and psychological

No, you're not going crazy.

- ◇ Forgetfulness
- ◇ Moodiness
- ◇ Anxiety
- ◇ Depression-like feelings
- ◇ Sensitivity to noise or light (yes, this surprised us too!)

GETTING AHEAD OF THE WAVE

The first step to wrapping your arms around your shifting hormones is to ask your doctor (either an internist or a gynecologist) to do a full blood screen for hormones, and then you'll continue doing this annually. Your FSH (follicle stimulating hormone) levels can indicate whether you're in menopause, as well as turn up information about vitamin deficiencies, cholesterol, and your thyroid function.

"As soon as you get past forty-five years old—everyone says, 'You're ready to join the menopause club!' And I'm like, I don't want to be in THAT club!! I just want to believe I'm having a stomachache from the candy corn I ate last night!"

Caroline, 46
SOUTHFIELD, MI

◇ Exercise regularly. It's been proven that just thirty minutes per day of activity in midlife can ward off or even prevent the onset of heart disease, diabetes, Alzheimer's, and colon and lung cancer.

◇ Eat well. You know this. But it matters more now than ever before. Our shifting hormones cause us to lose iron, gain weight, and generally zap our metabolism. Reducing sugar (not cutting it out entirely), lowering our overall calorie intake, and keeping an eye on our nightly glass(es) of wine will make a big difference.

Soften the edges

◇ Meditation

◇ Mindful breathing

◇ Experiment with the harder stuff—hormone therapy (check with your doctor as there are risk factors to consider)

◇ Progesterone cream

◇ For many women who have passed the stage of perimenopause and are in the full-on show, taking estrogen is the key to lessening hot flashes, night sweats, vaginal dryness, and a decrease in memory. You can also ask your doctor about other drugs on the market now for vaginal dryness.

◇ Bioidenticals, a natural type of hormone therapy

◇ The Pill (Yep, full circle, ladies)

And that's just the beginning. Considering that we all know what's inevitably coming, is there anything we can do to smooth the waters?

> True Confession:
>
> *"I smell now. All of a sudden I'm wearing men's deodorant. I'll be in a yoga class and smell someone—and realize it's ME."*

MIDLIFE HEALTH RISKS—WHAT TO KNOW AND DO

Beyond what we can outwardly feel at this stage, there are a number of lesser-known but long-term health risks menopause—and all the hormonal changes it entails—brings with it. Most notably, the loss of estrogen is a major contributor to heart disease in women. According to an article "Perimenopause, hormones, and midlife health," in *Harvard Women's Health Watch,* "our risk for heart disease only begins to zoom up when ovarian hormones start sliding into retirement." The other major risk we face now is osteoporosis, which is why it's so important to have a healthy diet, rich in calcium, and to exercise regularly, strengthening our bone mass.

In addition to exercising and eating right, it's critical to stay on top of the following regular exams:

"It feels like this storm in my body that's about to erupt."

Farrah, 49
CHARLESTON, SC

What to do	When to start	Recommended frequency
Mammogram	40	Annually
Pap smear	Ideally, you've been doing this all along	Annually
Colonoscopy	50	Every 10 years

One taboo health topic that kept coming up was an increased risk for eating disorders. We're losing control over our bodies and looks, we're facing down fears and anxieties about getting older, and just like that, the weight management techniques we've been using for decades just don't work. Many of us can revert back to unhealthy teenage behaviors we outgrew long ago.

WAIT—IT'S NOT JUST US??

One thing we heard from women we spoke to was how surprised they were to learn that their spouses or partners were also going through their own hormonal business at this time. At this phase in their lives, men's estrogen levels rise and testosterone levels drop. Their hormones are going just about as haywire as ours. And the shifting of their estrogen and testosterone levels has serious effects on men—which is something you rarely hear about! On a physical level, as their testosterone dives, many men gain abdominal weight while struggling to gain lean muscle mass. Which explains the growing

"I was forty-seven when I started going through all of these changes, including the hearing thing. (My colleagues and I had to Google it to understand!) It's kind of huge, and I'm coming to the end of it now. I'm on hormone therapy, and overnight all of these symptoms went away."

Molly, 50
DES MOINES, IA

paunch. And on an emotional level, rising estrogen helps them feel more emotionally attuned. And some women notice even more effects . . . As one woman shared with us about her husband, "We were married young and we've grown up together, so we've always been in the same place in terms of aging. I recently told him to get HIS hormones tested!!! The sex drive, the snappiness—they deal with all that too."

MEET YOUR MENOPAUSAL FRIENDS

Wherever you are in this whole menopause mess—whether pre-menopause, perimenopause, full-on menopause, post-menopause, or perplexed about what's happening to you and where you are in it all—we invite you to find your community here. Listen to the honest voices of others, so we can all share wisdom, experiences, gripes, and even the occasional victory.

"Now when I get my period it's 'YAY I'm not in menopause!' vs 'Yay I'm not pregnant.'"

Siena, 48
LITCHFIELD, CT

"I'm definitely staring menopause in the face. I haven't started yet, but I seem to have all the other symptoms: very low testosterone, insomnia. A couple of years ago I was having a really hard time sleeping—I thought I was getting depressed. So I went and had my hormones tested. Turns out I needed thyroid meds and testosterone, and once I got them, I felt a LOT of relief. The ragey-ness subsided. Everyone has a different opinion about what to do about hormones: Does it cause breast cancer? Will it harm me?"

Debbie, 50 FAIRFIELD, CT

The themes we heard:

◇ We're savoring the moment (as long as it lasts).

◇ We're feeling some anticipatory fear and dread.

◇ We don't appreciate fearmongering women a few steps ahead of us trying to get us all freaked out.

◇ We are resigned about the inevitable.

◇ We're just wanting to get it over with and be on the other side.

The themes we heard:

◇ We're feeling strong and defiant. (We can do this!)

◇ We're super confused—nothing is happening as planned.

◇ We're resentful about the lack of communication and openness.

◇ We're relieved that certain solutions actually work.

The themes we heard:

◇ We're uncomfortable and unhappy.

◇ We're frustrated and lacking a satisfying scapegoat.

◇ We're thrilled when something actually works to make us feel better.

◇ Some days, we feel like badasses.

◇ Some days, we feel lost.

◇ Most days, we're hot and pissed off!

"I have an IUD, so I don't really know what's going on. I do think I'm post eggs. I definitely do need to look at my vagina and see if it's losing its plump! I need to go and explore that situation—and I think that would REALLY freak me out and send me into a tailspin. Not because it's not beautiful. But OMG, it's going to look older! I had a gray eyelash and I was like, 'What the F*CK is that??' I think a gray pubic hair would freak me out."

Samantha, 47 OAKLAND, CA

"I had no idea what was going on—I thought it was stress or depression, and it was very confusing! No one really wanted to talk about it. I asked my mom when she went through menopause, and she wasn't helpful at all. Getting all the bloodwork and finding out where I was with it was very helpful. I started taking bioidentical hormones, and it was a really big deal to me—menopause was kicking my ass! I don't understand why people don't want to talk about it. It wasn't making me feel like an old lady. It was just my body shifting. I actually feel stronger than I ever have, and I'm exercising and taking care of my body."

Sheila, 52 TRENTON, NJ

"Menopause gives you a kick in the pants, with all the emotional stuff. I've had bleeding before, I've had mood swings before—but not like this. I'm crying at the drop of a hat, and I'm being a freak. But I'm blocking and tackling it as it comes on. Women don't talk about it openly, and that's too bad. I will talk about it with friends; I'll tell them, 'Okay, I've been whackadoodle and taking meds for it,' and it's helping a lot, so don't be afraid to talk about it!"
Jennifer, 51 SACRAMENTO, CA

"I had been regular on the dot every twenty-eight days. I started missing periods. I went to my gyno. I was getting hot flashes. She said, 'You're too young; you're forty-four.' This December it will be two years since I had a period. And two times a day it feels like I'm in a hot oven baking to death. They last three to five minutes. It's hard to concentrate, and it's troubling. I'll burst into tears for no reason. And I do think I'm struggling with my weight—it takes FOREVER now to lose. I need to talk to my doctor, but I felt she blew me off. Now I need to just call and make an appointment with a new doc, but I won't do it."
Anne, 44 ATLANTA, GA

"The age thing is weird, but we're not as silent about things as our moms were. When I would feel a hot flash, I would try to appreciate that my body was working in a certain way and giving me certain sensations. And once I accepted that, I could say, okay, I'm IN this now, trying to be mindful about it."

Cheryl, 51 FARGO, ND

"It's overwhelming me a little bit—just feeling like how quickly my body is changing. I'm only in my mid-forties and it's been such a quick thing, with the wrinkles and skin. Your skin just starts to change. You're losing hair, you're stressed out, you're not sleeping, there are bags under your eyes. It all starts happening!"

Katie, 46 ATLANTA, GA

"Now it's miserable! I have hyperthyroidism. My body is in chronic pain and I'm chronically tired."

Mindy, 49 KNOXVILLE, TN

Post-Menopause

The themes we heard:

◇ **We're experiencing a newfound inner strength and resilience.**

◇ **We're proud of having done it differently from our moms.**

◇ **We're appreciative of the power of our bodies to weather through such drastic changes.**

The truth is, we can't help you with the symptoms. We've got nothing for the dry vaginas, the raging hormones, or those freaking hot flashes. All we have are words, your words. And by sharing them back with you and opening up our circle, we are letting everyone in on the open secret that we are all going through this together. No one is alone. And at the end of the day, we hope hearing about all this, in its full unvarnished truth, is just what the doctor ordered. Or at least, a pretty good supplement to some pills.

FIVE THINGS TO CONSIDER AS YOU
APPROACH MENOPAUSE

1. Open up to your friends. All those girlfriends you've been leaning on for years and years? Guess what, we're all in this together. The more we talk and share, the more we normalize and help each other feel part of a natural community.

2. Accept the inevitable. It's happening, either now or in the near future. Take the time you need to mourn the "you" from before, and then open up the door to what is coming.

3. Throw out your tampons. Whee! Bonus.

4. Embrace solutions. Whether taking hormones or trying out natural remedies, there are lots of options. Start talking to women you know and trust to see what is working for them. If you could research nursery schools, you can damn well research this.

5. Fire your doctor if they don't listen to you. 'Nuff said.

Is This Really the Only Husband I'm Ever Gonna Have?

(Expect a Midlife
Relationship Reset)

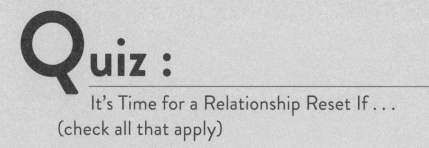

Quiz :

It's Time for a Relationship Reset If . . .
(check all that apply)

- When you hear the key turn in the lock, you pretend to be asleep (or pop an Ambien).

- The last time you had crazy good, memory-erasing sex there was a Bush in the White House.

- You eyeroll (to your kids) about your husband behind his back.

- When you're alone in the house, it feels like a spa vacation.

- Holding hands? Please. They only do that in the movies.

- Your recent crushes have included a friend's husband and/or a friend.

- You cruise OkCupid for cute older (or younger!) guys . . . and you're married.

- Sharing GIFs has dramatically improved your relationship.

- When you bring a date home, you pretend you have no food for the morning, so he leaves sooner.

- Your idea of being a "giving" spouse is tossing his socks in with your load of darks.

In our book *I'd Trade My Husband for a Housekeeper,* back in those early heady days of Phase 2, we spoke to more than 300 married women with kids. Of that group, 240—*that's 80 percent*—acknowledged that they could be happier.

Back then (as we heard consistently in our interviews), most of us were just slogging through it all. We'd come to grips with the fact that our partners were anything but perfect, we had established our tried-and-true scripts during fights that we could reliably turn to in a pinch, and we'd squared away our turfs. *I manage the bills; he deals with everything related to food. I schedule doctors' appointments; he schedules social appointments.*

For the married set among us, this wasn't working perfectly. But what did work was that women had a sense of shared purpose in getting through those challenging early days of colliding careers and kids' early lives. (Okay, most of the time.)

And for those of us who were single—whether single parents or single without kids—we were slogging through it too. We were headstrong in our prioritization of our careers, our achievements, and checking off those accomplishment boxes. All those crappy relationships we were accruing? They would all sort themselves out once we had the next job, next apartment, next therapist.

Newsflash: Here we are at Late Phase 2/Early Phase 3, and the slogging through is largely behind us. We're left wondering whether we're good with what we see in front of us. Are we okay, satisfied, happy, fulfilled, maybe even joyful with our relationships? *If not, what are we doing about it?*

At this point in our lives, we have the need to reevaluate the CRITERIA for who to surround ourselves with, the dynamics of these relationships, and who takes what priority:

◇ Partner

◇ Parents

◇ Kids

◇ Friends

◇ Siblings

As you look at the people you are surrounding yourself with, do you think they see you the way you see yourself? Are you happy with their reflection of you?

QUESTIONS WE'RE ALL ASKING:

◇ What community do I want to create/have I created? Am I satisfied with this community? What's missing/ what's positive or negative?

◇ What fears do I have about changing any of my current relationships? I may have a fear of time running out and needing to evolve. But what needs to shift?

◇ What are the key values I want to embody in my relationships? Examples: spirituality/thoughtfulness/ giving back/fun.

"We just didn't talk for five years because we had kids. Now it's like dating all over again. I just haven't seen him for five years. It's like a new boyfriend. Now we're looking at each other and saying, 'What is it that we want to do?'"

Kelly, 46
JACKSONVILLE, FL

THE STATE OF OUR UNIONS

First, let's all take a deep breath and look at the cold, hard, unsexy facts of the matter: what is the state of *our* unions? Here are modern facts from the Pew Research Center and the National Bureau of Economic Research:

Record Numbers of Americans Are Staying Single

Today, 20 percent of Americans ages twenty-five and older have never been married, compared with just 9 percent in 1960. That means the rate has more than doubled in the past fifty years.

The likelihood that a never-married adult will get married after age fifty-four is relatively small. In 2012, 71 out of 1,000 never-married adults ages twenty-five to thirty-four got married. The rate dropped to 40 per 1,000 among never-married adults ages thirty-five to forty-four, 16 per 1,000 among never-married adults ages forty-five to fifty-four, and only 7 per 1,000 among never-married adults ages fifty-five and older.

When We Are Getting Married, We're Doing It Later and Later

As of 2014, the median age at first marriage was twenty-nine for men and twenty-seven for women—the highest in modern history.

The "Untraditional" Family Is Becoming the Norm

Unmarried women accounted for 41 percent of births in 2011, up from 5 percent in 1960.

The rate of people ages eighteen to twenty-nine with stepsiblings is nearly double (44 percent) that of

"Now my husband and I are trying to concentrate on talking about US and our future—we've been trained to only focus on the kids! What happens next? Now we could move to Colorado and I could sell essential oils and be a HIPPIE!"

Tracey, 39
FAIRFAX, CA

their older friends, ages fifty to sixty-four (23 percent). Meaning: remarriage and/or blended families is becoming increasingly common.

Divorce Is Actually Less Common Than You Might Think

Divorce is less likely today than it was thirty years ago. The divorce rate today is 3.6 divorces per 1,000 couples per year.

Meanwhile, Those of Us Getting Divorced Are Increasingly Doing It Post-Forty

In 2014, people age fifty and above were twice as likely to go through a divorce than in 1990, according to the National Center for Family & Marriage Research at Bowling Green State University in Ohio.

And When We Do Divorce, It's Largely Our Decision

According to the AARP, about three in five divorces that take place after age forty are initiated by women.

Wherever you fall on this spectrum (single parent, unmarried, recently divorced, happily married, unhappily married), one thing holds true. We are all learning as we go; we have no consistent model for how this is supposed to work. And we all feel equally perplexed, and perhaps lost.

So what are we to do? We can start by listening to each other, cutting ourselves some slack, and being generous with ourselves and our partners. From there, we can hopefully determine how best to rebuild our relationships for the next half of this journey together.

> "We will each apologize within thirty minutes of an issue—it's our rule—and we move on. We each take turns— it's not just one of us."
>
> Carrie, 46
> HARTFORD, CT

CHOOSE YOUR OWN RELATIONSHIP ADVENTURE

We realize women in all manner of relationships are reading this, and we respect that we're all facing slightly different issues. So consider this chapter a "choose your own adventure." Find the community that speaks to you on the following pages, and we'll all meet up again in the friendship stage, page 165.

◇ **(Largely) fulfilling long-term relationship: Start below.**

◇ **(Largely) unfulfilling long-term relationship: Start on page 152.**

◇ **Single, whether newly, staunchly, sporadically, or reluctantly: Start on page 161.**

START HERE IF . . . You are in a (largely) fulfilling long-term relationship.

Congratulations. You are a rare and wonderful breed. Chances are good you've worked hard to be here. You've come out the other side of identifying your sources of inner peace and fulfillment, and you've attended to your marriage as an equally important part of your life. We all know that having strong relationships takes consistent work. Here are habits and behaviors to keep up, based on research, science, and time-honored nuggets of wisdom we heard from women around the country.

Think "we" not "I," and seek out new things together.

It might seem innocuous, but couples that use "we" (instead of "I") are hands down more likely to be happier. Robert W. Levenson, a professor of

> "When I go out to dinner with my husband, I silently mouth a fairy tale to him so it looks like we're actually speaking."
>
> Mali, 38
> CHARLESTON, SC

psychology at University of California, Berkeley, tracked 156 middle-aged and older couples over twenty years, revisiting them every five years. He discovered one simple difference between happy and unhappy couples: Couples that use "we" and "us" versus "me" and "I" are happier. Why? They feel more emotionally supported and have a shared purpose.

And finding the perfect shared purpose is just as important in determining what level of happiness couples experience. While "date night" is a good idea, heading to the same old spots, ordering the same old glass of chardonnay, and hitting the same old theater isn't going to help strengthen your bond as much as you might hope. The real secret to a successful date? Doing something new together. Scientists studying the brain have discovered that the happiest couples do things that are NOVEL and that they both are equally interested in. Tara Parker-Pope published a story on this topic, "Reinventing Date Night for Long-Married Couples," in the *New York Times* citing the work of Arthur Aron, a professor of social psychology at the State University of New York at Stony Brook. According to Aron, "new experiences activate the brain's reward system, flooding it with dopamine and norepinephrine. These are the same brain circuits that are ignited in early romantic love, a time of exhilaration and obsessive thoughts about a new partner."

Follow your own relationship script.

Every person is different. Every relationship is different. It's important to measure yourself only against

> "I'm proud of my marriage. I'm grateful that we're still able to grow together. There's a lot to look forward to with him. I will miss my kids a lot when they go to college, but I will really like having our time back. I can't wait to go to the movies ALL THE TIME!"
>
> **Amy, 50**
> Avalon, CA

your inner barometer, not anyone else's. If that means you like being away from each other 75 percent of the time, go for it. Tune out the inner (and outer) judges.

Be clear about who does what.

No one wants a tit-for-tat, scorekeeping kind of relationship, but it turns out that sharing household chores is a measure of successful relationships (along with faithfulness and regular sex). According to a 2007 Pew Research poll, 62 percent of adults of all ages and both genders said that sharing household chores is a very important measure of a successful relationship.

Get to bed!

Whether for sex or sleep, tucking in early is a major relationship strengthener. Bumping up your sex frequency from once a month to once a week increases your happiness as much as getting paid an extra fifty thousand dollars a year, according to research in a paper titled "Money, Sex, and Happiness" published by the National Bureau of Economic Research.

And once you're done, get thee to bed. People who sleep more tend to feel better about their relationship and report having fewer problems.

Argue honestly—and wrap it up.

Turns out the short-term agita of fighting is actually good for your relationship, as long as the conversation is open and honest.

> "'Five by five' rule—if it's not going to matter in five years, don't spend more than five minutes being upset about it!"
>
> **Darla, 49**
> DAYTON, OH

Last but not least, make a conscious choice to be happy in your relationship.

No one said this was easy. You, of all people, know the work it takes to continue to be generous and thoughtful and loving. Having a happy relationship is a choice you make.

Now, go to page 165.

START HERE IF . . . You are in a (largely) unfulfilling long-term relationship.

You started off strong. You were hot for each other, had some silly fun, grew up some, and now you find yourself HERE. It's not really what you'd imagined for yourself. You're frustrated, angry, alienated, lonely, and/or largely unfulfilled.

It's actually normal for relationships to act like an organism and evolve over time. What started as hot turns into overheated. You felt butterflies; now he makes you feel batsh*t crazy (and the feeling, sad to say, is mutual).

Dr. Laura Carstensen, a professor of psychology and the director of the Stanford Center on Longevity, has done a lot of work studying women at this stage and their relationships. "Just as with happiness, marital satisfaction follows a U-shaped curve as well, related to kids. Most couples are happy after their wedding, and then eighteen months after the birth of their first child things get rocky. And then STAY rocky until the kids leave the home!"

She notes that the issues leading to the relationship stressors are consistent: resentments over division of labor and financial pressures. "With the presence of kids in the relationship—even in an equal relationship—women tend to do more of the labor, and that tends to cause problems with the husbands. Husbands also feel left out and more pressure to earn more money and be successful."

Sure enough, we consistently heard several themes from women we spoke to about what frustrates them in their long-term relationships:

"We're essentially just co-parents and roommates, triaging our lives."

Some couples are basically just coasting by, ticking off the weeks, months, holidays, and milestones. In the face of all the obligations, you've become housemates more or less, passing ships cruising along. Unwilling to consider divorce, you're trying to find a way to make it work. Dr. Kathlyn Hendricks notes that the business of life can get confused with the business of your relationship. "This can become a source of leakage for the passion in the relationship," she explained to us. "People get into routines and suffer a deadening of the possibilities; it's just the same old, same old. We had a client who told us he knew his marriage was over when upon coming home from a business trip, instead of saying hello—his wife said, 'The upstairs toilet is broken again.'"

"I'm so tired of taking care of him. It's my time."

When we spoke with women who had chosen to split with their spouses, it was often because they realized their needs were just not being met. At a time when we are awakening to our own needs,

> "If you ask my husband, who I've been married to all along, 'Have you felt connected to your wife for the last five years?' he will say, 'Yes! Everything's great!' In reality, it's not great. We have both been just trying to survive this last handful of years."
>
> **Kelly, 46**
> JACKSONVILLE, FL

expectations, and dreams, this becomes increasingly unfulfilling and sad! After years—or decades—of triaging *his* needs, we come to realize that we need to make ourselves much more of a priority.

"We're stressed about money and it's all-consuming."

As you and your partner head into the peak earning years, reality sets in as to what your financial picture looks like now and into retirement. Maybe one (or both) of you has dealt with a layoff that set you back more than you'd planned. More than likely, major expenses loom: health bills, college, home repairs. And who better to take the stress out on than your partner. Financial sh★t has gotten real, real fast. And it's stressful!

"We're playing new roles and have less and less in common."

It's very normal to shift roles multiple times in a marriage. One person supports the other through graduate work, and then post-graduation, the roles shift. One person loses a job and becomes the primary peanut butter sandwich maker and laundry folder in the family. Talking to our friends, this feels like standard fare. But we still don't necessarily have a model to follow with our parents, who had more traditional trajectories for the most part. One woman lamented that the old model of women as primary caregivers in the home simply doesn't ring true to her: "Only 2 percent of ads show men doing housework. I'm no better at laundry than my husband!"

"I woke up one day and felt a shift. I had been taking care of him emotionally for so many years—and I realized that now it's time to take care of ME. I just didn't have the emotional capacity or space to do this anymore."

Liv, 45
WACO, TX

What's trickiest about all of this is that as our roles shift, we can feel increasingly disconnected with each other. Our new identities are unfamiliar to even us, and we can feel like strangers, at a loss for what to talk about at a painfully awkward dinner date.

"Thinking about sex (with my partner) fills me with dread."

Do you have it? Have you mourned it? Do you want/need to rekindle it? Do you know how?

> True Confession
>
> *"I opened my own bank account. I thought to myself, my god, if something happens to him, I don't know his passwords! I better open my own account so I can survive before I can figure all that crap out."*

Ten, twenty years ago, you and your girlfriends would get together and dish over drinks about what happened the night before. Now . . . not so much. Sex with your long-term partner is something you know (*yes, you know!*) is important for maintaining the strength of the relationship, but it's hard to make yourself feel it when you're so disconnected with him in other ways.

Some of us feel like we've lost our sex drives, and his constant taps on the shoulder are a source of

"For date nights, I only hang out with other couples so I don't have to have a real discussion with my husband."

Jenny, 47
PEORIA, IL

conflict. "I don't feel like I need someone to have sex with because I really don't care about it and that's fine. My sex drive is not that strong anymore. I have a lot of my married friends saying, 'When is it going to STOP?'"

Meanwhile, we're discovering our own selves, tapping into our own sources of happiness, and igniting our own sexuality in powerful new ways—and they don't always align with our partner. One woman told us: "I loooove sex, but I have not wanted to have sex with my husband for years. So I have a great vibrator and a great imagination. For me to be with him when the emotional connection isn't there makes it hard for me to then say, 'Let's get crazy in bed.'"

> True Confession:
>
> *"I have Skype sex with my Australian ex-boyfriend on a monthly basis. It's graphic and thrilling and makes me feel incredibly vibrant, and I don't regret a single second of it." (She's married.)*

"Suddenly no one is talking about sex! Now there's no excuse for not having sex—the kids used to be the excuse . . . now you have more time, you can focus. And there's so much at stake in our relationships now. I would've talked about any guy I was screwing in my twenties to my friends. Now, if you talk about it casually, it feels uncomfortable. I don't want soccer moms talking about my marriage. There is a very small circle of people you can talk to about your deepest, darkest stuff, but that's it. I wonder how many of us are dealing with a segmented emotional life!"

Samantha, 48 PORTLAND, OR

HAPPIER RELATIONSHIPS, STARTING NOW

The good news? There is some! Dr. Laura Carstensen of the Stanford Longevity Center notes that the stage we're at is precisely when things are primed to take a turn for the better. "Marriages actually return to honeymoon feelings after the kids leave! There's a lot of HOPE for afterward."

You've been doing so much work—starting with *reading this book*—to understand yourself, gain clarity about the stage you're at and what you're feeling, and figure out how to feed your soul now and into the future. It can feel like just one more item to add your relationship to-do list. And yet there are some fairly simple actions you take to invest in your relationship. By spending time nurturing your partner and relationship, you'll learn whether your investment will pay off with happiness, or if you're putting good money after bad—and you'd both find more joy in another situation.

Myths About Modern Marriage

If you have an affair, the marriage is done. Full stop.

A good marriage means you're happy all the time.

You're not supposed to fight.

Marriage starts strong and peters out.

He's more likely to cheat than she is.

Being in a relationship leads to greater happiness.

Staying together is good for the family.

You should share everything (finances, friends, inner secrets). If you don't, that's a bad sign.

Kids should always come first.

FIVE EASY INVESTMENTS TO MAKE IN YOUR RELATIONSHIP

1. Reconnect with your empathy

You're not the only one facing inner upheaval. Midlife affects men too—and not just in the clichéd ways we've all heard of (red convertible, new girlfriend, newfound respect for meditation). While it's culturally more acceptable for women to be in sync with what's happening to them, it's less common for men to bond with each other and share their journeys, which is especially challenging at a time when they've never been more ready to seek help and advice. As Gail Sheehy explores in *Understanding Men's Passages: Discovering the New Map of Men's Lives*, instead of feeling the kind of pain women do over losing our youth, men look at the transitions with dread. They don't know what to expect, and they're fearful of what's coming.

And for the most part, we're not paying great attention. One woman admits: "We haven't talked in five years—I have NO IDEA what my husband is going through! He could have a red Corvette out there driving around with five girls right now. At forty-five it's every man for himself! I'm not worried about him—he knows where to find me!"

But how can they adequately be there for us and support us if we're not paying attention to them? How can we expect emotional generosity from them if we look at them with anger or even envy? One woman was complaining about how her husband suddenly had a six-pack and it irritated her: "He looks hotter than ever and it's just not fair. How do you NOW have a six-pack? He does Pilates. I'm not happy for him. Not at all."

2. Take notes about what he's doing well

For whatever reason, men seem to have an easier time making drastic and important changes in their lives, forgiving themselves for what's not working and introducing new behaviors that serve them. We could learn from them here! And maybe join along, building up some novel, new, shared habits.

3. Get some action

This should not be news to you, but it's still important to remind ourselves. Sex is a critical part of a healthy relationship. People who have more sex are happier with each other. Authors and researchers Gay Hendricks, Ph.D., and his wife, Kathlyn Hendricks, Ph.D., assert that with counseling, couples can rekindle even a dead sex life—and create the best sex they've ever had.

4. Be reasonable—in both directions—in your expectations

He's been saying it to you for years, and dammit he's right. Part of the biggest gift you can give to your relationship is to be realistic about what is possible. Is your marriage going to solve every inner problem you've been wrestling with since you were twelve? No. Is your marriage going to make you happier? Only if your expectations of what is possible are on

"Here's my secret to a happy marriage: He always wanted to have sex more than me. I said if you leave me alone for two nights, I'll gladly have sex with you the THIRD night! And it slowly moved from two to three to four. It takes away the angst and disappointment."

Lana, 51
RYE, NY

target. No one's marriage is perfect; no one is perfect. Dr. James McNulty, a professor of psychology at Florida State University, conducted a study titled (no joke) "Should Spouses Be Expecting Less from Marriage."

As McNulty said in a statement, "Some people demand too much from their marriages because they are requiring that their marriages fulfill needs that they are not capable of achieving, whether because they have limited time, energy, effort, or skills to apply to their marriage. Other people demand too little from their marriages. Their marriage is a potential source of personal fulfillment that they are not exploiting. Ultimately, spouses appear to be best off to the extent that they ask of their marriages as much as, but not more than, their marriages are able to give them."

> "Newsflash: I became so much happier when I realized that my husband is not—and will NEVER be—my girlfriend!"
>
> **Tessa, 48**
> CHARLOTTE, NC

> *True Confession:*
>
> *"I like to smoke pot once in a while. It really helps with sex."*

A good place to start is to think about what your goal is for your relationship. Is it happiness? Support? Fulfillment? A successful partnership? In many ways, the bar has been set very high for our generation. We are told we have to be everything to each other. Soul mates and lovers and friends and more. But strip that away and ask yourself: what defines a "happy" marriage—for the two of you?

5. Do ONE thing differently

Kathlyn Hendricks is a fierce proponent of a super simple technique to improve relationships. She's seen it work time and time again with clients. "Just change one thing," she instructs us. "Maybe you change the time that you always have dinner. Maybe the wife always cooks and the husband helps make dinner one night. Just change *one* thing. When you pull that thread, things will start to shift. It wakes up the relationship." She says the fact that it's only one thing helps ensure that it's not an overwhelming shift. But once you're comfortable making one small change, you'll be even more comfortable making more new choices together as a couple.

START HERE IF . . . You're single, whether newly, staunchly, sporadically, or reluctantly.

Given that we've learned that previously untraditional relationships are now the norm, you're in very good company. More people are choosing to stay single later—and forever. More people are having and raising babies on their own. And perhaps most notably, more couples are divorcing at later stages. In fact, one quarter of all people who get divorced now are over fifty. Susan Brown, a researcher at Bowling Green State University, calls it the "gray divorce revolution." In a study, she writes, "the weakening norm of marriage as a lifelong institution coupled with a

"I do feel a sense of panic, to be honest, because time is going so fast and I'm not getting any younger. But here I am pressing the reset button on my personal happiness. I have feelings of fear—I don't want to wake up and find that my daughter is going to college and so I have to get a cat! I worry that I'm aging out of being marketable to men!"

Shauna, 47
STUART, FL

heightened emphasis on individual fulfillment and satisfaction through marriage may contribute to an increase in divorce among older adults, including those in long-term first marriages. Marriages change and evolve over the life course and thus may no longer meet one's needs at later life stages."

All of this is to say that there are no rules anymore. Yes, to be single and getting older is scary for a lot of us. We heard so many beautiful, smart women express fear and dread about being alone now.

At the same time, other women we spoke with were somehow recognizing that their relationship status was a conscious choice they were making—and one that was helping them be happy. We talked to several women who shared epiphanies that were freeing to them.

I Never Should Have Gotten Married in the First Place— Now I'm Doing It "Differently" and Proudly

The good news here is that as the norm shifts, there's less pressure to act or be a certain way. Getting divorced, not getting married, having a piece on the side. Nothing should be all that surprising. The key is to be comfortable with your own choices, whatever they may be.

I'm Not All That Interested in Dating

The whole model for dating today is different (Tinder, Bumble, whatever app du jour). What's more significant is how it fits into your life and agenda, which may be completely complicated in ways you hadn't even anticipated. We talked to newly single women trying to start dating who were mostly finding it to be a pressure, another thing on the to-do list. And if that's the case, it might be the universe saying the time is just not right. After all, if putting up an online profile is a recipe for stress, imagine how it might feel when someone you're into chooses to keep swiping right—on to other people.

I Still Need to Figure Out Who I Am, On My Own

For many newly single women, the hardest part can be figuring out who you are as a single person, not as part of a couple. This is not easy and it can be especially painful or lonely when a loss is still raw. But as we're stripped down to our essence, it's also an opportunity to reconnect with friends and find parts of ourselves that we'd previously ignored.

> "I don't think that I need to meet someone to make me whole anymore."
>
> **Marla, 43**
> NASHVILLE, TN

> True Confession:
> *"I don't want anybody to live with me*
> *EVER AGAIN!!"*

Bela Gandhi is the president of the Smart Dating Academy, a Chicago-based matchmaking service, which specializes in working with people over the age of forty. She has been called the fairy godmother of dating and prides herself on not only finding matches for people, but having zero divorces come out of matches she's made in her eight years of operating. The two keys to dating at this stage, she says, are 1) opening yourself up to partners you might have ruled out, and 2) being patient with yourself and others. As Bela tells us, "The way we're choosing partners—we're relying on instincts that have been pre-baked into us. Society has evolved and the expectations of what a 'good partner' looks like for you needs to shift."

Through an exercise she calls the "Marriage Map," Bela asks clients to make two lists. The first is qualities in a "dream guy." The second is a list of people in your life who make you really, really happy, the people who elevate you. What are the qualities that THEY have that might be different from those on list number one? Once you start to think about dating with a more expansive lens, everything can open up. "It's like your entire life you've been walking around with the wrong prescription glasses. All of a sudden, different people start to come into focus for you. Your pool gets much wider." While there are no promises, she says, the one certainty is that "love in midlife will come to you in an unexpected package. He's not going to be who you think he is. I hear people say all the time, 'I would have never looked at this guy before.'"

Then, once you begin dating, keep referring back to your list of core values you cherish. Keep being honest with yourself about whether people are delivering on your goals and needs. Whatever is on your list of values—"She's always there for me," "He makes

> "Before, when you were married, you made friends with couples. Now it's a whole new process again. You have to get to know who YOU are now."
>
> **Corinne, 53**
> STANTON, OH

me laugh," "He's got my back always," "She's a great listener"—should be present in your relationship.

Most important, Bela says, don't be thrown off by chemistry, whether you have it or you don't. "Sometimes butterflies are a warning signal—not what we should be searching for!" And on the flip side, she warns, "Lust is nature's trick to attaching ourselves to one person. Chemistry can come later—we've seen it happen."

RENEWING THE BONDS OF FRIENDSHIPS

While we are discovering as we go what we want out of our romantic relationships now and into the future, we are all clear on one thing: our friendships have never felt more important to us. (And we're talking real, physical, in-person relationships, not just "likes" on a picture and "friends" in a feed.) This is a time of friendship renewal and reawakening. For many of us, it's as if our friendships have been in hibernation, and we are craving our oldest, dearest friends with a newfound vigor. Part of this happens because as we are increasingly sure of ourselves and confident in our own inner compass, we have the conviction and desire to reach out and hold tight to each other's hands. And perhaps most important, we've shed the layers of people who we now realize don't lift us up.

Kerry, a married mother of two boys in Milwaukee, Wisconsin, has come to treasure her longest-lasting friendships, and she believes you don't need to be surrounded by crowds of friends to feel the love. "If

"A woman I know did a vow renewal with her husband. And my friends were like 'Are you f'ing kidding me? That is so stupid.' What we SHOULD do is a friendship vow renewal!!! And that's what we're gonna do next summer for our girls' weekend— in Vegas!!"

Sarah, 52
STUDIO CITY, CA

you're lucky, you have two really good girlfriends who last with you through time. I love knowing women who have known me through various phases in my life." That time-honored knowledge becomes even more valuable as the years pass.

Kathy is a newly divorced mother of three in Bardstown, Kentucky. Her youngest is seventeen, her marriage is over, and her house is quiet. And with all the space, silence, and unresolved emotions, she's more eager than ever to rekindle her relationships with old and new friends. "I'm really looking forward to fostering my friendships now."

While the two of us are, ourselves, old and dear friends, we also have learned how making new friends at this stage can be especially rewarding. We're all at a place in our lives where we're comfortable in our own skin, we're confident about who we are, and we know ourselves in a much more succinct way. Coming from such a spiritually sound place like that allows us to connect with other women much more easily than we ever have. We know what we want, we know what we don't want, and we know a good friendship when we see it.

At a time when marriage may be downshifting, our lives and families may be taking new shape, our inner selves are blossoming, and our friendships are hitting a new stride. And it couldn't be more important to us. Female friendships stand alone in their uniqueness and benefits. They are the result of choices we make, which lends a certain amount of wonder and open-endedness that allows for exponential curiosity and growth.

> "This is the one thing I feel is so important for us. Ultimately what do you have in your life? Your parents die, your kids leave you, your husband could leave you, but what are you left with? Your girlfriends. There's nothing quite like girlfriends."
>
> Mallory, 51
> BOWIE, MD

DOUBLING DOWN—ON THE RIGHT FRIENDS

You know those friends that aren't completely *friends*? They make you feel kind of crappy about yourself—but they've been in your life for over a decade so you keep them around? We're clearing out the weeds and saying goodbye. We're now asking ourselves: does she lift me up or drag me down?

One woman we talked to, Jenn, has a "no asshole" rule that she implemented in her late thirties. Whereas she once would let a few people slide into her circle who didn't make her feel great, those people no longer make the cut. Another told us, "I know that I feel wiser and more discriminating in the kinds of relationships I want to embrace now. I'm not just going to grab anyone and go party like I used to."

"Surround yourself with people who like your kneecaps just the way they are."

Rene, 49
AUSTIN, TX

FRIENDSHIPS WITH BENEFITS

Yes, your girlfriends back you up when you're worried you've made the wrong choice in a couch—or career. Yes, they show up when there's a terrifying health scare. And yes, they bring a bottle to pop when a kid gets into college. All around, true friends help with self-confidence, support you through change, and celebrate the good stuff.

But the benefits go far beyond that, which is why it's so important that we're making friendships a priority in our lives, now more than ever. We're navigating all this new stuff, in parallel paths, and it's time to invest in and tap the community we've built up over the years. As two friends ourselves, who turn our lives upside down to make sure we talk every single day without fail, we know firsthand the immense joys of friendship.

And it turns out that neuroscience has some pretty compelling evidence supporting the fact that the power of friendship—whether with old or new friends—maintains brain health and well-being as we get older.

FRIENDS DO THIS FOR ME TOO?

Improve memory

Having a healthy social life naturally involves thinking, feeling, sensing, reasoning, and intuition. These mentally stimulating activities build up our reserve of healthy brain cells and promote the formation of new connections, or synapses, between neurons.

Neuroscientists often talk about "cognitive reserve." Cognitive reserve refers to how resilient the mind is to damage or decline of the brain. Think of it as a savings account for the functionality of our brain. It's the ability to build up a resistance to mental decline and disease.

Reduce risk of dementia

Neuroscience research shows that being socially connected protects the brain against the risk of developing dementia. Women with large social networks (note: this study was conducted in person and didn't even include Facebook friends!) have a lower risk of cognitive decline as they age. Why? Loneliness is associated with more than double the risk of developing dementia.

"My two close girl-friends fill me in a way that no man could. There's zero judgment, they support me no matter what, and we share an unspoken 'knowing.' We joke about living together in a sisterhood commune when we're old and gray (or before that)!"

Amy, 48
RENO, NV

Here's how loneliness and lack of social connection compares to more well-known risk factors. Feeling lonely long term can lead to the same risk factors as:

◇ **Smoking fifteen cigarettes a day**

◇ **Being an alcoholic**

◇ **Not exercising**

◇ **Obesity (twice as harmful!)**

Brigham Young University Professor Julianne Holt-Lunstad, lead author on a 2010 study, "Social Relationships and Mortality Risk," says, "When someone is connected to a group and feels responsibility for other people, that sense of purpose and meaning translates to taking better care of themselves and taking fewer risks." Another of the authors, also from Brigham Young, Professor Timothy Smith, points out that modern conveniences and technology can lead some people to think that having a tight network of real, live friends isn't necessary. "We take relationships for granted as humans—we're like fish that don't notice the water," Smith said. "That constant interaction is not only beneficial psychologically but directly to our physical health."

Lengthen your life

Those good friends of yours are worth nurturing, because friends will help add a few years on to your life. A meta-analysis of 148 studies, including 300,000 people studied over seven years, found that people with strong social relationships had an increased

"I realized recently how isolated I'd become. I work from home, so I could go days without really interfacing with the outside world. I just joined a collaborative workspace and it's like natural Prozac—I'm SO much happier! I love being around other creative people, and it's the community feeling that really fills my soul."

Aimee, 39
RUMSON, NJ

likelihood of survival (yep, they were less likely to die) than those with weaker social relationships.

YOUR RELATIONSHIP WITH YOUR KIDS IS *QUICKLY* SHIFTING

We've talked about our partners; we've talked about our friends. But our relationships with our kids, if we have them, is also entering a new stage. How are they evolving as they're aging and we're aging?

First off, it's important to acknowledge that the relationship we've had up until now is not necessarily the one we're *meant* to have at this stage and into the future. Our kids are breaking off, asserting their independence, sorting out who they are separate from us. That's 100 percent their job right now. And our job is to support them in that endeavor.

We have to make a conscious choice to look at them through the lens of their leaving and becoming independent. We still need to parent them and guide them. It's hard work; it takes time and effort. It starts with considering our kids as budding adults, deserving of a new kind of attention. We have to ask them about their feelings, listen, and not judge. It's tough to break out of generational patterns we're familiar with. If we didn't necessarily have close relationships with our parents, how do we navigate building a better model with our growing children?

Begin by asking yourself these questions:

◇ **When is the last time you asked them how they felt about a situation?**

◇ When is the last time you apologized for your behavior?

◇ How do you think they would describe themselves as people?

◇ What are they passionate about?

◇ How do you think they would describe you?

It can be helpful to start to think about them as more fully formed people, with legitimate thoughts and feelings worth exploring. From there, it's important for us to try on some new behaviors with our kids.

Dos and Don'ts for Engaging with Your Kids Now and from This Day Forward:

◇ When they walk in the door, DON'T accost them about homework, what happened to them over the course of the day, who they ate with at lunch, etc. Do *you* like that?

◇ DO think about what skills you can share that would serve them well. Folding laundry? Properly washing a dish? Setting up a bank account?

◇ DON'T immediately try to solve problems for them. Ask them what they think they should do, talk through possible solutions, and counsel them through pros and cons. Your job right now is not to push away obstacles, but to help your kids learn how to navigate them on their own.

◇ DO help them get organized, and remind them about what they need to do—without nagging. Nagging will make it seem like the task they need to complete is for you and it will set off an oppositional dynamic. Instead,

"I realized that my job isn't to be the 'cool, open-minded mom.' I thought I was building a close relationship with my twelve-year-old daughter by letting her make her own rules, but in reality she was silently begging for more structure."

Cindy, 38
ORLANDO, FL

"My relationship with my teenage son shifted the minute we went on a volunteer trip together. We created an experience that changed our lives forever—and one that no one else can understand but us. Now there's a warmth that's new and wonderful."

Karen, 39
HARTFORD, CT

try to make them create systems where they remind themselves (e.g., using a whiteboard, writing notes to self, setting up app alerts).

◇ DO engage in new experiences with your kids—whether it's taking a class together or taking a trip solo with one of them.

SEVEN SIMPLE STEPS TO STRENGTHEN RELATIONSHIPS

1. Practice feeling more empathy for your partner and your kids. Put yourself in their shoes, and think about what their experience is in a particular situation. Are they feeling worried, vulnerable, unsure? Why not ask them?

2. Make happiness a goal. You've set ambitious goals for yourself in your career and your inner self. Happiness can be the ultimate ambitious—AND attainable—goal in your relationships. Set an intention that you want to prioritize fulfillment, contentment, or shared well-being.

3. Invest in your friendships. If it's been too long since you've made a big "deposit" in your friendship bank, consider a friendship vow renewal with your closest girlfriend(s). Set a date, book a house rental, order a case of wine, and make it clear to all that you are committed to each other for better or for worse, for richer or poorer, in sickness and in health, and till death do you part.

4. Focus on the positive. Be mindful about what you have together that is working. When your partner says something, you could choose to interpret it any number of ways. Do your best to filter everything through a positive, generous lens.

5. Default to "we" instead of "me." In your language and your actions, be as mindful as you can about prioritizing the relationship. Be present when you are together (put down the phone). Just even using the word "we" will make you feel more connected to each other.

6. Level-set your expectations. Let go of too-high or false expectations for what you think is a "good" or "perfect" union.

7. Have sex tonight. Get high if you need to. Just do it already.

Don't Be Afraid to Fail, Be Afraid Not to Try

(Discovering Your Purpose and Passion)

Quiz :

I'm Grateful for . . .
(check all that apply)

- The ability to take deep breaths and feel what it does to my body.

- The fact that I'm still here—and, for the most part, healthy.

- Not knowing what will happen tomorrow and being okay with that.

- Living in a place where, whatever my political views, I'm allowed to believe whatever I want.

- A super-strong, squeezy hug.

- The sound of loud, unabashed laughter.

- Liking myself more today than I did yesterday (or maybe last month).

- Old friends who truly know me and love me and all my quirks.

- ◆ The ability to help other women feel good about themselves.

- ◆ My solitude.

- ◆ A perfect soy latte, and the slow 15 minutes I take to savor every drop.

- ◆ Innate faith that everything is going to work out, one way or another.

- ◆ The ability to make new friends.

- ◆ The LACK of drama in my life—consistency is comforting!

- ◆ Truly giving zero f*cks about what others think of me.

- ◆ The ability to say "Why NOT me?"

- ◆ The tough times in my life, because they've made me who I am today.

Throughout this book, we've shared our deepest inner confessions, acknowledged what's new for us in this generation, and opened our minds to what's possible as we head off onto the next phase. And now, here and now, is the time when we are open, raw, and ready to accept all that's possible for us. Anything can happen, any day. We are free and newly confident and accepting of ourselves—limps, warts, wiggly bellies, weird habits, perfectionism, and all.

Now is the time for us to pop our heads up after a lot of hard work in careers and raising kids—and reevaluate and reimagine what is truly meaningful to us. Suddenly, there's no beginning and end to our lives. We graduated from school, built careers, got married, raised kids, adopted pets. Now, when the kids are leaving and your career is what it is, the beginning and end points get fuzzy. Having a passion, a purpose, or perhaps a passion that creates a sense of purpose can create a new sense of meaning in our lives.

Sure, we don't have the security of being young anymore. But that security is a double-edged sword: it comes with certain fears, obstacles, and risks. When we are younger, we are fearful of the implications of our actions. *If I take this job, will I be happy in five years? Is this who I am? If I marry him, am I ready to commit for fifty-plus years?* With decades stretching ahead of us, we are less willing to jump into new things because it feels like the decisions we make have unknown and interminable implications. What we choose to do somehow feels like it is decisive and permanent.

That is no longer the case. Our choices and actions still have implications, but they feel more temporary. We have the wisdom of our years and knowledge banks we've built up. We have inner trust and faith. We also see sliding doors slowly closing but still leaving us room to get out and explore. Our prevailing mantra of the day has become: Why not? And why not me?

Bela Gandhi, the matchmaker in Chicago, was someone who completely pivoted from one career path to another after allowing herself to acknowledge her true passion and purpose. While she'd always had an instinct that she had a knack for figuring out how to make successful matches between friends, she ultimately did what she was supposed to and joined her family business.

Only when she got a call from the first couple she set up did she let that little voice in her head gain volume. At that point, she was running the family business and raising a five-year-old and a one-year-old. "I was SO nervous—what are people going to say? Matchmaking??" Tuning out the voices, she put a business plan together and started down this path. "My parents are Indian immigrants from Bombay—and the land of arranged marriages! It was crazy to them." But Bela stayed strong and consistent in her pursuit, attending conferences, putting a resume together, and taking on clients, one by one.

> "We dole out advice to our kids, but we don't apply it to ourselves. We need to listen to our intuition — what feels right? What's truly motivating us?"
>
> **Raina, 38**
> PEORIA, IL

So how do we reinvent parts of our lives, make room for the next chapter, and embrace what comes next? It starts with getting in touch with our purpose and passion, learning to be appreciative, grateful, and maybe just a bit more present.

"I had a huge career, and last year I just decided to leave it all. I was making a huge amount of money. I had worked my ass off my kids' whole childhood. But I wanted to experience Seth in his last year at home. And now, I'm puzzled; I'm gonna be around another forty years. I have to keep myself busy—in a meaningful way. And I'm feeling like, 'What's next?' I've LOVED the last year of being free, not checking my email. I realize I'm so lucky, but I also think that I'm missing having an active mind, being useful, being social, and all of that. And at the same time I'm feeling a lack of energy to be proactive about it. I'm floundering a little bit. I've never had this moment of 'what now?' I feel a little stuck. I always had one career path."
Sarah, 52 STUDIO CITY, CA

I'VE DONE IT ALL; NOW I NEED TO HAVE A PURPOSE TOO?

Even talking about finding our purpose can feel self-indulgent, decadent, ungrateful. After all, if you're here reading this book, chances are you're at least fairly successful, mildly interesting, and somewhat healthy. At the very least! Chances are you're in even better shape than that. So shouldn't that be enough?

It is totally all right—and even normal—to feel that it is not.

Several years ago, we found ourselves asking just that question. "Is this it? Is this all? What is next?" We had written our first three books, and we were not sure what lay ahead of us, what we were meant to be doing with ourselves. Everyone else seemed to have ideas, but we were just processing other people's expectations, instead of understanding what we felt we should—or wanted to—do. We didn't really know what our path was meant to be, what our ultimate goals for ourselves were. We were also unable to feel truly settled in the moment. We were somehow still "hungry" despite having accomplished what we'd set out to do. And that, alone, left us feeling like we had important internal work to do.

We set off on our own path seeking answers, which we did together. Our path involved so many different actions. We worked with spiritual guides, shamans, healers, each other, and on our own. We worked, really worked, to understand what lay beneath our feelings, and to visualize what we hoped to achieve. Ultimately, we came to understand that we wanted to help women through our work, both through our books and our company. We believe that we have a responsibility to share our journey and build community and greater understanding. And we honestly couldn't have gotten to this place without each other and without committing to the work of digging deeper within ourselves.

We continue to do our mindfulness work together every single day. It has undoubtedly benefited us, and

"I don't want to waste any more time. I look back and realize how wonderful those moments with our kids were. We did these amazing road trips—so simple, and not fancy. We had great times. It all comes down to gratitude, and I want to find that again."

Miriam, 49
Annapolis, MD

we are firm believers in the power of visualization to help create a new course in our lives. You can call it whatever you like, but it is work, and it is perhaps the most important work we can do for ourselves at this stage in our lives.

PATHS TO TRY TO DISCOVER MINDFULNESS

Whether you're more into Reiki or running, any number of methods have been proven to help people quiet the mind, discover their passions, and build healthy habits that guide them into the future:

◇ Meditation

◇ Energy work

◇ Reiki

◇ Hiking

◇ Therapy

◇ Breathwork

◇ Visualization

While we should all be grateful for what we have, at this moment in our lives, it's our JOB to start taking care of ourselves, to nurture our own souls, and to rekindle our own inner flames. It's okay to feel the thirst for more. The most important work we can do is to rediscover what makes our own hearts sing.

Growing up we often had "passions" handed to us, expectations about what we should or could be good at. We spoke to so many women who were essentially

"My kids are still my number one priority—but now, it has to be about me, too. They're moved out! They're grown-ups. What about me? Even my kids tell me I need to find my own happiness."

Ruth, 55
GREEN BAY, WI

told from a very early age what they were good at (and what they weren't). And consistency was key. You want to be a teacher? Great. *Learn, teach, stay the course, retire. And . . . cut.*

Our parents didn't have the permission to ponder their paths and passions. And so we are uncomfortable searching for our own paths—and we're not even sure what it is meant to look like. Moving careers multiple times, much less making bigger changes in your life at this stage (getting divorced, discovering a new side of your sexuality, going back to work for the first time since your kids were born, taking a pole-dancing class, or learning guitar), well that just wasn't something you did, much less contemplated in a public way.

We feel alone both in our search for more choices and in our feelings about wanting them at all. Said one woman, "On the career front, no one told me you're in charge of your own destiny. If you want to get something done, no one will swoop in and do it for you. You have to take ownership of your own life. Be the positive person in the room. No one else is going to do it! Take it by the reins. In my career I always thought I'd have a mentor to help me."

But instead of looking at this as a selfish choice, you can choose to see it as healthy modeling—for your kids, for younger women, for anyone paying atten-tion! By allowing ourselves the permission and license to layer something else in our lives, we are teaching everyone around us that we value making meaning-ful choices, and they can too. This is not selfish. It's impactful and important.

> "There's a little shame around not knowing what you want to do. 'Really? Why haven't I figured it out; everyone else did! She started this thing, that start-up. . . .'"
>
> Karly, 39
> HINGHAM, MA

Jon Rasmussen, the shaman and author of *Dreaming Your World into Being,* stresses how critical it is to the entire family—not just you—to take this time to reinvest in yourself and rediscover your passions. "It's more than just giving yourself permission to work on yourself," he notes. "This is your *obligation*—for yourself, your relationships, and your kids. We're paving the path for them, allowing them their own freedom. I'm seeing women trying to move to another phase, and yet they're hanging on to their kids as their identity. You need to be free, so that they can be free in turn. Ninety percent of everything is learned by example, subconsciously or not. So if kids see their mother doing this transition as early as when they're thirteen or fourteen, that sends ALL the right messages—this is what it means to be an empowered woman."

CHOOSING THE RIGHT PASSION OR PURPOSE IS A PRESSURE

So, *ready, set . . . connect with your passion!* Ha, if only it were that easy. Not sure what your passion is? What fills your soul? As common as that is, our lack of clarity and connection with our passion can make us feel self-judgey . . . critical . . . maybe even concerned.

And once we acknowledge that we are hungering for something more, we can judge ourselves for not really knowing how to fill that void. You might not have any idea what to do, what excites you, what you could be passionate about. As one woman contemplated the question, she wrestled with it and started

"There's a saying I love which I use as my mantra: 'Don't be afraid to fail; be afraid to not try.' If more girls and women used that as their mantra, we'd all go a lot further. I don't want to be afraid to fail. I want to try and do as much as I can. When you lose that burden of failing, when you stop caring about what other people think of you, the sky is the limit. There are plenty of women out there who judge me, but I really don't care."

Jennifer, 47
CHAPPAQUA, NY

to judge herself, comparing herself to others: "What's my purpose? I don't even know what that means. Those kids leave—but they're such a huge part of my identity. I look back and regret my choices. I could be doing something creative and cool."

The fact is, many of us are not super in touch with what brings us joy. We know what we're good at, where our talents lie, but there's a big difference between where we've excelled and the activities that make our hearts sing. Maybe you've been a stellar real estate agent your whole life. Closing that next deal is electrifying. Putting families in homes they love fills you with joy. You're great at it! People have been telling you this is what you've been meant to do your whole life.

Is that your passion? Is it why you've been put on this Earth?

As a super-high-achieving group, we're constantly evaluating ourselves and our statuses. So it's no surprise that for many of us, the first thing we think of when we begin to consider "passion" and "purpose" is to connect it with prestige, title, or money. "Purpose" is a huge word and it can paralyze us—and prevent us from uncovering where we're supposed to be. It can feel lofty, weighty—a recipe for applying even more pressure on ourselves. *I have a career, a family, a good life. Now I need a purpose, too?*

"It's funny—I always knew exactly WHO in my life brought me pure joy—but it wasn't until I discovered WHAT brings me joy that I figured out my true calling. I love to help people on the front lines. I finally got the courage to apply to nursing school. It's the hardest thing I've ever done, but I have a smile on my face every single day!"

Jaime, 39
SAN DIEGO, CA

HOW THE HELL AM I SUPPOSED TO KNOW WHAT MY PASSION IS?

The first step? In our personal journey to discovering our path, we had to start by taking a deep breath and cutting ourselves some slack. We didn't know what we were driving at, and we had to start by being okay with that. That was maybe the hardest part. Over time, we worked to visualize our intentions, understand our deepest goals, and stay focused and faithful on working backward to make our intentions a reality. It was—and continues to be—hard work! But once we gave ourselves room to breathe, and to practice self-love and acceptance, we made space to feel deeper emotions, including gratitude and peace. It continues to be something we work at every single day, together and on our own.

One thing that truly helped us was getting outside of our worlds and our comfort zones, making ourselves uncomfortable and purposefully opening our eyes to things. It's all too easy to wallow about where we've been, what's passed us by, and yes, even our bygone bikini bodies. All that starts to feel awfully small when you force yourself to do something new, whether it's getting a hobby or maybe even traveling to a place where people are *lucky* to have extra flesh on their bodies.

Kathlyn Hendricks, the author of *Conscious Loving*, believes the first step to uncovering new perspectives and sources of passion is to start with self-appreciation.

"I got this silver watch for being at my marketing firm for fifteen years. And I'm thinking, 'Does this even mean anything to me?' I've been stuck in the same routine for so long I hadn't ever stopped to question it. I mean, I'm good at what I do—and I feel accomplished—but it's not filling my soul in any way. There's a voice telling me to figure it out, but I don't even know where to start."

Tessa, 40
SAN ANTONIO, TX

"That is the gateway to loving yourself. Start by noticing and being willing to find ONE thing you really appreciate about yourself," she told us. "I like to have people look in the mirror and say it to themselves, or write it in a journal. You have to express it in some way, to wake yourself up again. All you need is ten minutes a day where you focus on what it is you most love to do. What is it that, when I'm engaged in it, makes time disappear and leaves me feeling nourished? It doesn't have to be profound, but doing it makes you feel creative."

Questions to ask yourself:

◇ What feeds your soul? Gardening? Riding horses? Drawing? Swimming? Reading novels? Connecting people?

◇ Ask yourself, what brings you energy, what fills you up? A talent is what you expend energy on; a passion is what mobilizes you and propels you forward.

◇ What truly brings you joy? Who brings you joy?

◇ What would you do if you felt absolutely no judgment?

◇ What if you didn't care about mastering something, and you could learn something just for fun?

◇ If you had to set an intention for the next ten years, what would you like that to be?

One very concrete way to figure out your passion is to create what former Google career coach Jenny Blake calls a "mind map." Start by writing down the year in the center of a piece of paper and draw a circle around it. From the circle in the center, extend

> "I have to be bold and brave. I don't know what the next phase is. There's still a lot of life left and I didn't envision this other part—what comes NEXT. I feel like for the first time I'm becoming myself. Not a daughter or a wife. I am bubbling at the surface now. It's just ME."
>
> Shelly, 49
> CHICAGO, IL

spokes. At the end of each spoke, write goals that are important to you, whether it's increasing family time, more reading, focusing on your health, rebuilding your marriage, finding ways to be more creative, etc. From each spoke, draw out additional smaller spokes with very specific actions you might take to realize those goals. For example, if more reading is on your main spoke, your smaller spokes might read, "join a book club," "sign up for Goodreads to get recommendations from friends," and "talk to a voracious reader I know to get recommendations." As Blake explained to CNBC, mapping everything in such a visual way allows you to be both specific and open-minded. "The goal is to break out of linear thinking," she says. "Go broad. Go big. Go sideways, and then experiment to see which of your ideas is most likely to lead to a resonant next step."

Jon Rasmussen suggests that it's helpful to think back to a time when you were a preteen or teen. "You have to reclaim that awe, that naïveté, that belief that 'I can do anything I want!'" He asks: When you had time to play, what were you drawn to? What did you do? What did you get excited about? "As young beings, we're purely in touch with our souls' primary desires," he tells us, "and it's usually the most obvious simple things that bring you joy." He says that the best first step is to list the silliest little things you used to do as a kid. For example, his wife used to set up a chalkboard and play school with her dog or anyone else who was willing. For her, that was it! "If you're wondering what you want to do now, this exercise will

"I went to law school, became a lawyer, and eventually admitted to myself that I hated it. I went back to school at thirty-nine to become a psychologist. Looking back to when I was younger, it was so obvious—I was always that person who my friends turned to for advice, for help. I loved helping people sort through their emotions and come up with solutions."

Nina, 44
SPOKANE, WA

probably lead you there," he says. "You can extrapolate and interpret it—and get reclaimed by life again." If you made mud pies in the dirt, maybe you actually do enjoy baking and would feel great joy from learning how to make bread.

IT'S SORT OF EXHILARATING AND TERRIFYING

Once you give yourself license to uncover your passion, it's an exhilarating, freeing, and perhaps terrifying thing to recognize. But this is the time to face down those fears. "Birth is a painful experience, and now this process is similarly painful," notes Rasmussen. "It's a huge reboot of your entire being. I think it's important to recognize that pain is part of this process. It's about loss and grief, too. It's all part of it."

It can feel like we only have one shot now. This is it. We cannot let fear hold us back. And so often it does! What are we afraid of? The list can go on and on:

◇ I'll fail.

◇ It's too late for me to take up a new hobby.

◇ People will think I'm silly.

◇ I'll be seen as selfish to take time for myself.

◇ I won't actually enjoy that thing I think I'm passionate about.

◇ I'm too busy to actually commit. I'd love to open a store, but I'm just dealing with too much right now.

◇ It would take me away from more important things I should be taking care of.

"I wanted to leave my career in real estate to try being a stand-up comic! But I was so freaked out about what everyone else would say that I didn't even talk about it for three years. Last year I started taking improv classes, and I just did my first stand-up routine. Even though I was scared, I can't even tell you how much joy that brought me—but I STILL didn't invite my friends and family!"

Ava, 41
LOS ANGELES, CA

But the truth is, if not now, when? We have to look at our dreams and goals and passions separate from the perfect storm that surrounds us. If we look outward, we will see that we have so many resources and so much support from the people around us.

"I knew I was supposed to be doing something new and different but didn't know what it was," said Lisa Rueff, humanitarian and creator of Sparked, a game intended to connect, inspire, and uplift people. "I got invited to a dinner party with these incredible dynamic women and we were going around the table sharing our intentions and dreams. We shared what we needed help with in our current journeys. I drove away, and wow! I thought, how can I create this inspiring feeling among people? I started sketching out my idea for Sparked right then and there."

Maria is someone who did a career about-face at the age of forty. By all measures, she was successful. She was a stockbroker in Toronto, and she had as much money as she could want. But when she started being really honest with herself, she realized that the career she had been building for herself wasn't making her happy. Money wasn't enough. It was time for her to actually admit that, and make a change. So, she looked deep inside and discovered that she'd always been interested in working in television. She quit her job, got her bachelor's in journalism, and took an internship on a show, at the very bottom of the totem pole, getting coffee—at forty. Over many years, she slowly but surely worked her way up. "I eventually became a producer and was producing a show with a mentor who was twenty-five!"

"I've learned what I DON'T want to do. It's nice to know that about yourself and take that stand. I'm a process person. I found a job where I can do that. And I don't have to babysit people."

Rene, 49
AUSTIN, TX

> "I thought, 'I have to do something for me.' I decided to run the NYC marathon—and I had never exercised a day in my life. I used running as a metaphor—if I can do this, I can do anything. Not only did I run, I ran with a torn meniscus. It was the best twenty-six miles of my life."
>
> **Kelly, 46**
> JACKSONVILLE, FL

It was unquestionably scary for Maria to start at the bottom—again. But she ultimately found that putting herself in a vulnerable position, being around coworkers nearly half her age, and being a novice, was part of what made the experience work for her. "It gave me vitality and energy being around younger people."

What unifies all these stories of women making meaningful and important changes in their lives is one thing: an attitude. Charles Swindoll, a prominent non-denominational preacher in Texas, has a lot to say about the power of a positive personal attitude: "Attitude, to me, is more important than facts. It is more important than the past, than education, than money, than circumstances, than failures, than successes, than what other people say or do. It is more important than appearance, giftedness or skill. . . . The remarkable thing is we have a choice every day regarding the attitude we will embrace for that day. We cannot change our past . . . we cannot change the fact that people will act in a certain way. We cannot change the inevitable. The only thing we can do is play on the one string we have, and that is our attitude. I am convinced that life is 10 percent what happens to me and 90 percent how I react to it. And, so it is with you . . . we are in charge of our attitudes."

RUNNING FOR THE HILLS—NOW THAT'S A SIGN OF PASSION

You know that crazy girlfriend who weirdly picked up running at the age of forty. She's always posting on Facebook about her marathons.

You and your friends teasingly ask her what she's running from. Well, she's onto something—even if she may not be aware of it.

Research shows that the effect of exercise on the brain and body is more powerful than we ever knew. And a brisk walk can be about as good as body building. Kirk Erickson from the University of Pittsburgh has dedicated his life to studying the effects of exercise and activity on aging adult brains. In a 2011 study, he found that, after a year of fast walking (forty brisk minutes a session), healthy adults between the ages of fifty-five and eighty saw the size of their hippocampus jump by 2 percent—compared to a 1.4 percent shrinkage in non-walking friends. That 2 percent jump in size can essentially add a year or two to your life, so it's pretty significant stuff.

THERE'S NEVER BEEN A BETTER TIME: TAPPING INTO YOUR PERSONAL DATA

Whatever you choose to do, whether starting a new hobby or a career, know that you've never been better equipped to take something on. At this point in our lives we've built up a great deal of internal data on ourselves. What makes us happy? What doesn't make us happy? What are we good at? What skills do we have that bring us joy? All of that information can be put to great use to propel us forward.

Research has shown that people in their forties are some of the most productive workers—in fact, the economy tends to grow faster when there is a rise in

"I realized that all of my kids' friends would come to my house because I love to cook and we always have a lot of home-made leftovers here. One day my daughter's best friend was helping me make a soufflé—and it dawned on me—what if I started a cooking class for kids? I started with just a small group, but it's been the most fulfilling part of my life!"

Macy, 39
HANOVER, MA

population between forty and forty-nine. The higher the ratio of people ages forty to forty-nine, the faster the economy increases its output per hour of work. As Jason Furman, former chairman of the Council of Economic Advisers under President Obama, hypothesized to *Bloomberg Businessweek,* workers in their forties seem to have "a good balance of experience and creativity."

At this stage, we've built up a reserve of knowledge, we've learned so many skills, and best of all, we've begun to ditch those unhelpful inner fears. All of that combines to make us efficient and creative. So knowing that, now really, what's holding you back?

PASSION-FINDING DOS AND DON'TS

DO: Start small.

Think of starting something new in terms of short-term goals and longer-term goals. Short-term goal: Learn the basics of cycling. Long-term goal: Enter a local race by the end of the year.

DON'T: Overthink it.

As thoughtful as our generation can be, don't be paralyzed by this as a "to do"—try something new, frivolous, silly, fun. And think about doing it with a friend, or a child (yours or someone else's)!

DO: Give it time to sink in.

Research shows us that passion can be sparked by trying something new, even if you don't fall immediately in love with it.

> "I'd love to be known as a great friend. A loving, present mother and wife. Someone who is kind and giving and who taught her kids important values."
>
> **Kim, 49**
> CHARLOTTE, NC

STRATEGIES TO TAP INTO YOUR PASSION AND DISCOVER YOUR PURPOSE

Embrace your curiosity

Albert Einstein once said, "I have no special talents. I am only passionately curious." If the man who developed the theory of relativity valued his own curiosity more than any talents he had, that's a pretty good endorsement for being wide-eyed and open-minded. Stay inquisitive about yourself (and others!), and continue to listen and learn about what makes you smile—and what your heart is telling you to back away from. You might just be surprised by what you discover tomorrow.

Revisit your core values

At any point in your life when you're "searching," the best action to take is to go back to your core values. That holds true now more than ever. If you find yourself deeply unhappy, or even slightly "off," chances are good that you've moved away from your core values. For some, one of those values might be compassion. For others, it could be your ability to solve problems. What are the things that are most important to you? What defines who you are? With every answer you discover within yourself, ask "why?" Why is that important to you? Why does that make you feel good? For example, instead of saying something like, "My kids are what is important to me," dig deeper to something such as, "I like to cook and make people feel good."

"I no longer feel that the perception of success from other people is important. I don't need to chase that anymore. My passion and my joy is important—rather than keeping up with others."

Briana, 37
SALT LAKE CITY, UT

Pick up a hobby, any hobby

We all need something to ground us. Whether it's spirituality, running, religion, or meditation, it helps to have something we do regularly to stay centered. We cannot feel guilty for taking care of ourselves—mind, body, and soul!

And if you need a good excuse here it is: Researchers at the Mayo Clinic in Minnesota tracked over 250 people in their eighties over four years, and their findings show that picking up a new hobby or skill or activity in your second half of life helps your body and brain as you age. And that holds true whether or not you're actually good at it.

Those who had picked up anything from painting to drawing to sculpting had healthier brain function and were less likely to develop mental lapses than those who didn't pick up any new artistic skills. Stimulating your brain, however you choose to do it, benefits you in more ways than one.

The power of setting an intention—and writing it down

Happiness doesn't just appear. Goals don't just get met. Values aren't something you're just impulsively reminded of. And your purpose is certainly not just going to slap you in the face one day with a vigorous *Voilà!*

It starts with you setting an intention. What does that mean? Signing yourself up for a change. Articulating to yourself what it is you'd like to see happen. You can write it down on a Post-it note, scribble on your bathroom mirror using a whiteboard marker, or send yourself a letter to arrive in three months. You could even put it into pictures, or make it come to life visually somehow.

The truth is, it doesn't have to be big. Sometimes a small intention can make the biggest impact. Sasha Korellis has spent decades working with herself—and other women—through meditation, yoga, and now jewelry she makes called Satcha Malas that can be used as meditation aids. She's noticed that our egos can get in the way of our ability to set an intention. "We think we have to do something BIG and MASSIVE. If we just do one small thing, it can make a big difference. Just a small gesture in someone's life. Experiment and dig deep—ask yourself—what is it that I really like to do? What would I do if I could not go to work today, and I stay home? Experimenting—and allowing ourselves the time to have that exploration—is key. It doesn't just happen. You have to find your tribe, and that can take two to three years."

Whatever you do, manifest your goals in order to make them real. The idea is to be able to look back later and use the documents as checkpoints or anchors, to revisit where you are, where you've been, and where you'd like to go.

When we started doing the hard work of figuring out our path, we set very clear intentions and dedicated all of our focus to visualizing them coming to life. For many women, their intentions at this stage can be clear, and oh-so-different from what they'd been in the past.

"Starting anything new can activate your insecurities. I'm working with women younger than I am. It's really easy to think you'll never catch up or be good enough. I went away the weekend before I turned fifty by myself, and I just decided that my intention for when I turn fifty is to erase the negative thoughts that take over, to let go of the negativity about who I am and where I'm going."

Melissa, 54
NORTHAMPTON, MA

Be open-minded with yourself

You never know when your inner voice will win the shouting match with the loud-ass voice in your head. For Annie, it happened one morning in the shower. "Your whole life you're waiting for inspiration in the shower! For me, it actually happened. My voice said I should be a therapist! That day, I decided." Part of what worked for Annie was when that voice came, she was ready to acknowledge it, accept it, and listen with an open heart and mind. "I've found that if you're clinging to where you were, you can't embrace what's next."

SIX SIMPLE STEPS TO DISCOVERING YOUR PURPOSE AND PASSION

1. Forgive yourself for not necessarily knowing Right This Second what it's supposed to be. You've had a lot going on over the past ten, twenty, thirty years. If you spend too much time thinking about what you're NOT doing, it'll be all the harder to unearth that happiness within yourself.

2. Trust your intuition. Listen to your heart. You know yourself better than you're giving yourself credit for. You've got this.

3. Rewind to your childhood. Don't remember much? Ask people who were around you then to help you remember making mud pies, pretending you were a teacher, etc. You'll find all your clues there.

4. Start small. A mile-long jog doesn't have to turn into marathon training. It is just that, a mile-long jog.

5. Embrace experimentation. Try something. You don't have to commit to any one thing. Swim today. Help kids learn to read tomorrow. Start walking a mile loop in your neighborhood next week. Nothing is permanent. Just listen to yourself and be respectful of the voice you hear back.

6. Be generous with yourself. You've spent so much time caring for others. You're a devoted friend, partner, sibling, child, mom, etc. It's your turn to be generous with yourself. And the ultimate act of generosity is to give yourself the permission to have a purpose now.

In Conclusion: A Passionate Plea for Gratitude

LET'S ALL TAKE A MOMENT TO JUMP IN THE GRASS

W e're at a time of opening, not closing. What unites us all is that we want this next phase—this next chapter—to be meaningful. So how do we do it?

It starts with mindfully changing our perspective. Often we think of this time as a time of loss—we're losing momentum in our careers; maybe we lost a job, lost our kids, lost our marriage; maybe we're losing passion for our everyday lives. How about looking at life through the lens of what we have? This is another way to talk about gratitude.

We've been running at warp speed for so long, if we do feel gratitude it's often fleeting because we move so quickly on to the next thing. This is the moment to take time to truly understand what gratitude means to us and what we're grateful for. Maybe, just maybe, it will help quiet your mind and allow you to unlock the path you're drawn to, the meaning you're meant to find.

One way to connect with your gratitude is to take five minutes at the end of each day to close your eyes, take deep breaths, and literally name everything you're grateful for. Write it down. The simple act of documenting what you're grateful for will create a sense of focus throughout your day, as you mentally flag things you'll want to write down. After forty days, gratitude will become more top of mind, more of a habit. Names, faces, and things will pop into your head on their own.

The two of us have a gratitude ritual we call a "jump-in-the-grass moment." Whenever we have

"I don't look at things like a LOSS. I see my girlfriends feeling loss with kids going to college, and I look at them and think, 'You're just lucky to have a child, a beautiful child who has options. And you need to step back and reflect on that. You're looking at this from the wrong lens.'"

Valerie, 55
SAN FRANCISCO, CA

something—big or small—to be thankful for, we literally find a patch of grass, run onto it, and jump up and down, in unison. Sometimes we're together, sometimes we're on opposite sides of the country, sometimes we're on a big lawn, and sometimes we make do by pouring out a potted plant. Whatever form the jumping takes, the point is to experience gratitude physically, in one perfect, shared moment. The ritual forces us to slow down, appreciate, celebrate, and take glory.

So maybe we should do a little grass jumping together here. We're grateful that you've joined us in this journey, that we are now part of the same like-minded community of women, that we are a new badass crew. We're grateful to the generations of women who came before us who paved the way to give us options and the vision to see them. We're grateful for our husbands and kids and doctors and friends and spiritual coaches and babysitters and neighbors. We're grateful for the hundreds of women who opened up their minds and looked into their souls to lay bare their fears, secret passions, and inner voices. We're grateful that you read this book with an open mind and open heart, which makes us all part of one community where we can all support one another without judgment. And we're hopeful that you have picked up a couple of thought-starters and solutions—or even just found some solace, relief, or a giggle over a shared confession or sense of community. We're grateful for you.

"Take a deep breath and get on the phone and call people you're grateful for. Whether it's a friend, a vendor, a colleague—let them know that something they did positively impacted you."

Victoria, 50-ish
MILL VALLEY, CA

"Here is a test to find out whether your mission in life is complete. If you're alive, it isn't."

Lauren Bacall

ACKNOWLEDGMENTS

To the countless women we interviewed for this book, thank you. Thank you for your honesty, your humor, your vulnerability and your insights. You are now part of a movement that will help lift this generation of women (of any age!) higher, without limitations, into their next chapters.

Thank you to our husbands and kids for your commitment and unwavering support (and crazy wide eyes when we told you that "Uh yeah, we're writing another book . . . !").

Sarah Malarkey at Chronicle—what a journey we've been on together, since you took a chance on us in 2004. Thank you for your incredible open mindedness and support. Amy Treadwell for loving this concept from day one and beautiful editing. Abby Hoffman, who believed and opened doors, Nina Willdorf, whose talent and enthusiasm is inspiring. Tracy Steinbrenner for being so solid throughout this entire journey! Jon Rasmussen, for your love, guidance, and "knowing" throughout our journey and over the years.

Eric, there is no one I would rather be on this life journey with, you are my rock and my love. Alex, Pierce, and Julia, you are the loves of my life. So grateful to be able to watch you spread your wings. I continue to learn from you every day. Val and Jerry Gibbons, thank you for teaching me to always to believe in myself and give it my all. Nancy and Larry Ashworth, thank you for being great role models for our marriage, your laughter is infectious.

Paul, thank you for so many years of support and love. Emily and Sam, my love for you is unconditional and boundless—and I cherish you each and every day. Phyllis Menken, your endless cheerleading is amazing. Kathy and Peter Nobile, you never cease to amaze with your support and genuine affection.

Sarah Pearsall (Sass), you have become a luminous light in my life and I am beyond grateful for you. Jenn Pearsall, we are all family and I cherish you. Shelley Mosby, the love never ends—no words needed. Caleb Hartzler, you are my Angel, always. Jason Press, thank you for supporting me and this book from the beginning. Brian Kelly, I am beyond that we found each other and share such a genuine love. John Fasulo, you matter. And I love you. Nora Clifford, your words and support have guided me so much. Keira Muller, soul sister always.

Millie Froeb, Tracy Brennan and Marsha Todd, thank you for being the best friends a girl could ask for. In the name of Sisterhood, I look forward to live on our commune and play cards at eighty. That will be the next chapter to look forward to, and I bet it will be a great one. Suzi Gurry, thank you for laughing with me and being authentic. I adore you.

For so many incredible souls who have been there for us with unconditional love: Hunter Cressman, Victoria Cressman, KK Sample, Rose Wells, Lisa Rueff, Jennifer Grove, Katie Giblin, Jenni Luke, Nancy Deane, Agnes and Henry, Mark Malinowski, Shauna Brasseur, Christy Salcido, Andrea Rothschild, Wendy Selig-Prieb, Kelly Burns, Christy Turlington, Ged Robertson, Julie Samuel, Freda Gu, Mike Lippert, Maria Bromley, Deena McCreath, Gail Pipkin, Ellie Andrews, Sasha Korellis, John Rasmussen, Nancy Ludwick, Jan Power, Peter Nobile, Cheryl Nobile, Michael Nobile, Alexa Price, Miranda Abrams, Nadine Berry, Hannah Hudson, Zoe Bonnet, Vali and Curtis Nemetz, Kiersten Cabalka, Grace and Steve Cabalka, Joe and Kristin Cabalka, Cristin and Scott Gibbons, the whole Gibbons crew, Lisa Becker, Brooke Anderson, Jodi Bricker, Annie Bjork, Debi Gollan, Toni Canada, The Terch Family, Renee Maka, Carie Betram, Linly Belshaw, and John Abbamondi.